Nantucket
RECIPES
From The Fog Island Cafe

NANTUCKET RECIPES

FROM THE FOG ISLAND CAFE

MARK DAWSON
AND
ANNE BLAKE DAWSON

CHAPMAN BILLIES, INC.
SANDWICH, MASSACHUSETTS

Fog Island Cafe

7 South Water Street
Nantucket, Massachusetts 02554

Published 1996 by

Chapman Billies, Inc.

P.O. Box 819
Sandwich, Massachusetts 02563

ISBN 0-939218-16-X

Production supervised by Jenna Dixon

Printed in the United States of America by BookCrafters.

Publisher's Cataloging-in-Publication Data
(prepared by Quality Books, Inc.)
Dawson, Mark, 1956-
    Nantucket recipes from the Fog Island Cafe / by Mark Dawson and
Anne Blake Dawson.
        p.   cm.
    Includes index.
    ISBN 0-939218-16-X
    1. Fog Island Cafe (Nantucket Island, Mass.). 2. Cookery, American.
I. Dawson, Anne Blake. II. Title.
TX715.D39   1996
641.5'09744'97   QBI96-40265

05 04 03 02 01 00 99 98 97   10 9 8 7 6 5 4 3 2

In loving memory of Jayne Taylor Blake,
mother and inspiration.
We will always listen to your
"silent words in the quiet of our hearts."

CONTENTS

INTRODUCTION

The idea to create a Fog Island cookbook first took shape after receiving countless recipe requests from our guests at the Cafe. Many of our customers kept saying, "You guys should write a cookbook!" Flattered by the support, we finally took the advice to heart.

In compiling this cookbook, we chose to include not only the most frequently requested recipes but also recipes that specifically use ingredients indigenous to Nantucket. Local favorites include Cranberry Oatmeal Cookies, Linguini with Nantucket Bay Scallops, Red Pepper Corn Chowder and Nantucket Fish Cakes to name a few. All the recipes included in this cookbook have been offered on our menus at various times.

We believe the dining public should be given healthy menu selections that incorporate nutrition and great taste into fine cuisine. Our menus offer many vegetarian and low-fat alternatives for our customers with specific dietary needs. Popular vegetarian dishes include Black Beans and Rice, Bamboo Steamed Vegetables, Roasted Veggie Hero, and a Grilled Portabello Mushroom Burger as an alternative to the all-American beef burger. Our goal is simply to offer a variety of menu choices with alternatives for everyone and to prepare every dish using proper culinary techniques to achieve outstanding quality in taste and presentation.

Hopefully, the publication of this cookbook will help you recreate some of the dishes you enjoyed while dining at the Fog Island Cafe. There is a mail order form in the back of the book, if you wish to order some of our specialty foods used as key ingredients in the preparation of various recipes in this cookbook. ✖

Thanks and Acknowledgments

We are truly grateful to our loyal customers who have supported us over the past few years and certainly owe our success to the tremendous reception we have received since opening day. Thanks again for your support!

We are equally indebted to our staff members, whose sincere dedication and hard work has been immeasurable.

Special thanks to Clara Urbahn for her encouragement and support. The illustrations in this cookbook are Clara's creations. In appeciation for her efforts, we wish to donate a percentage of the profits from this book to the Nantucket Antheneum Library on her behalf. ✖

I
CELEBRATED BREAKFASTS

Fog Island Cafe is probably best known for the award-winning breakfasts we serve. Breakfast by its very nature is an unassuming meal that rarely aspires to the limelight.

Because of this unpretentious quality and the fact that people love to be pampered in the morning, we make every effort to offer creative and wholesome morning meals prepared with a personal flair.

We want our guests to relax in a cozy comfortable setting and simply enjoy eating great food conversing with friends and family or reading the daily newspaper.

Baked Apple Pancake
Drizzled with Caramel Sauce

This pancake puffs up like a soufflé and
makes for a dramatic presentation at the breakfast table.

Yields 4 servings

INGREDIENTS

2 Granny Smith apples, peeled,
   cored, and sliced
2 tablespoons lemon juice
1/4 cup granulated sugar
1/2 teaspoon ground cinnamon
1/4 cup butter

3 eggs
1/2 cup milk
1/8 teaspoon salt
1/2 cup all-purpose flour
Caramel Sauce (see next page ↗)

METHOD

1. Preheat oven to 400 degrees.

2. Put apple slices in a large bowl
   and add the lemon juice, sugar,
   and cinnamon. Toss to mix.

3. Melt butter in a medium sauté
   pan or cast-iron skillet over
   medium heat. Add apples and
   cook, stirring frequently, until
   the apples are tender but still
   hold their shape. Remove from
   heat and spread apples evenly
   over the bottom of the pan.

4. Mix eggs, milk, salt, and flour in
   a blender until smooth.

5. Pour this batter into the
   skillet on top of the cooked
   apples.

6. Place in the preheated oven and
   bake for about 20 minutes, until
   golden brown and puffy. Check
   to make sure the pancake is
   fully cooked in the center by
   inserting a knife or toothpick—
   it should come out clean.

7. Prepare caramel sauce (see next
   page ↗).

8. Remove pancake from oven and
   turn immediately onto a warm
   serving platter, so the apples
   are on the top. Drizzle with
   warm caramel sauce and dust
   with powdered sugar. Serve at
   once. ✄

CARAMEL SAUCE

INGREDIENTS

¾ cup granulated sugar
¼ cup water
¼ cup heavy cream

METHOD

1. Place sugar and water in a saucepan and stir slowly to dissolve.

2. Cook over medium heat until the melted sugar begins to brown. Swirl the pan over the heat so the sugar colors evenly. Do not stir. When the sugar has reached a rich golden brown color, remove pan from heat.

3. Pour in heavy cream. The sugar may splatter and the cream will foam up dramatically, so move your hands away from the pan as quickly as possible. When the bubbling subsides, stir caramel sauce, mixing in the heavy cream completely.

4. This sauce will harden as it cools, so always serve warm. ✖

BREAKFAST BURRITO

This became such a popular morning special, we recently decided to add this dish permanently to our breakfast menu.

Yields 6 servings

INGREDIENTS

1 tablespoon clarified butter (see next page ✒)
12 eggs, cracked and beaten
½ cup scallions, sliced
6 large flour tortillas
1½ cups Fog Island Fresh Tomato Salsa (or substitution)

3 cups grated cheddar cheese
1 cup sour cream
1 cup guacamole (see next page ✒)
6 servings Spicy Black Beans (p. 82)

METHOD

1. Place a large nonstick skillet over low heat and add clarified butter (see next page ✒). Pour in eggs, add scallions and scramble until fairly soft. Remove from heat.

2. Warm tortillas individually in a large skillet but do not brown.

3. Preheat oven to 400 degrees.

4. Distribute scrambled eggs in the center of each tortilla and spread 2 to 3 tablespoons of salsa on top of the eggs. Sprinkle with a little grated cheddar and roll tortillas tightly, folding in the ends.

5. Place tortillas seam-side down on a sheetpan and sprinkle remaining cheese on top.

6. Bake for about 5 minutes, until the cheese is fully melted.

7. Serve with sour cream, guacamole (see next page ✒), and warmed black beans. ✖

CLARIFIED BUTTER

Clarifying butter is a simple process that removes the milk solids naturally contained in butter from the churning process. The elimination of the milk particles gives the butter a higher smoking point so the butter will not burn as easily when used for cooking. Once clarified, the butter can be refrigerated for three to four weeks or even frozen if desired.

Yields about 3 cups

INGREDIENTS

2 pounds butter (preferably unsalted)

METHOD

1. Cut butter into chunks and place in a heavy medium-sized saucepan.

2. Place over medium heat and bring to the boiling point, carefully watching to make sure butter does not boil over. Continue to simmer for 10 to 15 minutes longer.

3. Remove from heat and let stand for 30 minutes to an hour, until the foam on the surface of the melted butter subsides and the milk solids settle to the bottom.

4. Using a ladle, carefully skim the foam from the surface and discard.

5. Ladle out the clear butter into a clean storage container until you reach the milky residue on the bottom of the saucepan. These are the milk solids and should be discarded as well.

6. Store the clarified butter in the refrigerator until ready to use or freeze if desired. ✕

GUACAMOLE

This is a popular Mexican dish that we serve as a garnish for many dishes at the Cafe. If making ahead of time, keep in mind that avocados oxidize when exposed to air; the guacamole will turn a brownish color if left uncovered.

Preparing the dish as close to serving time as possible will assure a bright green color. If storing, cover well with plastic wrap and keep refrigerated. Do not add the salt until just before serving.

Yields 1½ to 2 cups

INGREDIENTS

2 large ripe avocados
1 teaspoon minced garlic
¼ cup minced red onions
¼ cup minced red peppers
2 tablespoons finely chopped scallions
1 tablespoon freshly chopped cilantro
½ cup sour cream
1 lime, juiced
¼ teaspoon salt
¼ teaspoon chili powder
Dash Fog Island Real Hot Sauce

METHOD

1. Remove the avocado from the skins and mash with a fork in a medium-size bowl until fairly smooth.

2. Add garlic, red onions, red peppers, scallions, cilantro, and sour cream and stir until well mixed.

3. Add lime juice, salt, chili powder, and hot sauce and stir well. Taste and adjust the seasonings as needed.

4. Serve immediately. ✕

BRÏOCHE FRENCH TOAST

This classic yeast bread recipe from France is fairly rich due to the butter and eggs used in making the dough. At Fog Island our French toast is prepared using this special bread, but you can easily substitute other breads such as Portuguese, challah, or French baguettes.

Yields 6 to 8 servings

INGREDIENTS

1½ cups half-and-half
¼ cup orange juice
4 eggs
2 tablespoons pure maple syrup
1 teaspoon vanilla
½ teaspoon grated orange rind
1 teaspoon cinnamon
½ teaspoon nutmeg
1 loaf brïoche bread (see next page ↗), cut into thick 1-inch rectangles and halved into triangles
¼ cup clarified butter (p. 6)

METHOD

1. In a large bowl, whisk half-and-half and orange juice with eggs until combined.
2. Add maple syrup, vanilla, orange rind, cinnamon, and nutmeg and continue to whisk until blended.
3. Dip brïoche triangles in the egg batter and let soak for at least 20 to 30 seconds, turning so the batter is well absorbed. Do not leave in the batter for too long or the bread will become soggy and fall apart.
4. Heat a large skillet or griddle over medium heat and brush liberally with clarified butter. Place the soaked bread on the griddle and cook until bread is a golden brown on the bottom, about 1½ to 2 minutes. Flip and continue to cook almost equally as long on the second side. Repeat process with the remaining slices, adding clarified butter to the griddle as needed. Keep cooked French toast in a warm oven while the additional batches are cooking.
5. Serve with warmed maple syrup and whipped butter. For a more festive breakfast, top with fresh berries.

BRÏOCHE BREAD

Yields one loaf (8½ x 4½-inch pan)

INGREDIENTS

1 tablespoon or 1 package active dry yeast
½ cup warm water
2 tablespoons sugar
1 cup butter, melted
1 teaspoon salt
4 eggs
4 cups all-purpose flour
Egg wash: whisk together 1 egg, 1 egg yolk, and 1 tablespoon water

METHOD

1. Dissolve yeast in the warm water and stir in sugar. Let sit for about 5 minutes.

2. Add melted butter, eggs, salt, and flour and knead the dough just until a smooth ball is formed. This is a fairly soft dough.

3. Cover the dough and let rise in a warm spot for an hour or so, until it has doubled in volume. Punch the dough down.

4. Turn the dough onto a lightly floured surface and roll into a ball. Keep the dough covered and let rest for 15 to 20 more minutes.

5. Press down the dough with the palms of your hands into a rectangular shape. Roll the dough tightly with the heel of your hands, tucking in the end so the loaf is even. Pinch the edges and place seam side down into a lightly greased loaf pan.

6. Let the dough rest in the pan for about 45 minutes, until the dough rises 1 inch over the top of the pan.

7. Preheat oven to 350 degrees.

8. Brush with egg wash and score 3 slashes across the top of the loaf using a sharp, serrated knife.

9. Bake for about 45 minutes. To test for doneness, when the brïoche has reached a golden-brown color, carefully remove from loaf pan and tap gently with your fingertips. The tapping should produce a hollow sound. When done, remove from oven and turn onto a rack to cool.

CHICKEN HASH FOG-STYLE

This unusual dish is one of our signature breakfast items. We received a letter last summer from Gourmet magazine requesting a copy of this recipe, which we happily provided. We were thrilled when our recipe was included in the October 1996 issue.

Yields 6 servings

INGREDIENTS

2 tablespoons clarified butter (p. 6)
1 cup onions, diced
½ cup green pepper, diced
½ cup red pepper, diced
1 tablespoon garlic, minced
½ teaspoon salt
1 teaspoon paprika
½ teaspoon black pepper
½ teaspoon white pepper
½ teaspoon leaf thyme
½ teaspoon chili powder

4 cups chicken meat, poached*
  and diced
3 cups red bliss potatoes, boiled
  and diced
½ cup scallions, sliced
½ cup parsley, chopped
1 cup light cream or half-and-half
12 eggs, poached
6 to 12 slices whole-grain bread,
  toasted

METHOD

1. Melt butter in a large sauté pan or skillet over medium heat. Add onions, peppers, and garlic and cook until tender, stirring frequently.

2. Add the salt, paprika, black and white pepper, thyme, and chili powder. Cook for one minute to toast the spices. Stir in poached chicken meat, potatoes, scallions, parsley, and cream. Taste the hash and adjust seasoning to taste.

3. Continue to cook, stirring occasionally, until the cream reduces and the hash becomes golden brown. Flip the hash over and brown the other side as well.

4. Remove from heat and portion onto warmed serving plates. Top each serving of hash with two freshly poached eggs and serve with toast. ✖

* To poach chicken, bring 4 cups chicken broth or water to a boil in a deep 12-inch skillet. Add 2 whole skinless boneless chicken breasts (about 1½ pounds) in one layer. Reduce heat and allow to simmer gently, turning once, for 7 minutes. Remove skillet from heat and cool chicken in cooking liquid for 20 minutes. Transfer chicken to a cutting board, discarding liquid, and cut into ½-inch cubes.

EGGS BENEDICT

One of the key ingredients of an outstanding Eggs Benedict is
the hollandaise sauce used to top the poached eggs. It is well
worth the time to make this classic sauce from scratch.
The preparation is not as intimidating as many believe.

Yields 8 servings

INGREDIENTS

16 thin slices of ham or Canadian
   bacon
8 English muffins, fork-split and
   toasted
16 eggs, poached

1 batch hollandaise sauce
   (see next page ⬈)
Fresh dill sprigs for garnish
   (optional)

METHOD

1. Prepare hollandaise sauce (see
   next page ⬈).

2. Place ham in a small skillet and
   brown lightly. Cover and keep
   warm while the English muffins
   are toasted and the eggs are
   prepared.

3. Place 2 toasted English muffin
   halves on each warmed plate.

Cover each half with a slice of
ham, then carefully place the
poached eggs on top.

4. Spoon 3 to 4 tablespoons of
   hollandaise on top of each
   serving and garnish with a sprig
   of fresh dill. ✖

HOLLANDAISE SAUCE

INGREDIENTS

6 egg yolks
2 tablespoons water
1 pound clarified butter,
    warmed (p. 6)
1 lemon (juice from)
Salt and dash of Fog Island Real
    Hot Sauce, to taste

METHOD

1. Whisk egg yolks and water together in a small stainless-steel bowl until frothy.

2. Place bowl over a pot of simmering water (similar to a double boiler) making sure the bottom of the bowl does not actually touch the water.

3. Whisk yolks continuously until cooked to a soft peak. Be very careful not to overheat or the eggs will become scrambled. If the eggs appear to be getting too hot, remove the bowl from heat and let cool for a few seconds before returning to the heat. Once a soft peak is obtained, remove the bowl from the stove.

4. Slowly pour clarified butter into the eggs, whisking continuously until the butter is incorporated and the sauce has thickened.

5. Add lemon juice and season with salt and cayenne pepper to taste. ✄

VARIATIONS

Substitute different ingredients in place of the ham for creative alternatives:
    California Eggs Benedict
        with spinach and grilled tomato
    Eggs Oscar
        with crabmeat and asparagus
    Irish Benedict
        with corned beef hash

FLUFFY BUTTERMILK PANCAKES

These pancakes are fabulous! . . . about as light and fluffy
as you will find.

Yields about 18 large pancakes

INGREDIENTS

2 cups cake flour
½ cup whole wheat flour
¼ cup granulated sugar
1 teaspoon salt
3 tablespoons baking powder

2 eggs
1 cup milk
1 cup buttermilk
3 tablespoons butter, melted

METHOD

1. In a large bowl, mix together the flours, sugar, salt, and baking powder.

2. Add eggs, milk, buttermilk, and melted butter and stir until blended, being careful not to overmix. This pancake batter is fairly thick and will still have some small lumps after combining.

3. Heat a griddle or skillet to medium heat and grease lightly. Spoon out about 3 to 4 tablespoons of batter per pancake onto the griddle.

4. Cook until a few bubbles break on top and pancake is firm around the edge. Flip pancake over and cook until golden brown, making sure the center is fully cooked. Total cooking time is about 3 to 4 minutes. Serve immediately with softened butter and warmed maple syrup. ✖

VARIATIONS

Fresh fruit
   Always a wonderful addition. Serve either on top of the cakes or mixed with the batter and grilled to taste.

FRESH STRAWBERRY CREPES

Crepes may be filled with either sweet or savory fillings.
When strawberries are in season, these are a great addition
to a Sunday brunch menu.

Yields 8 servings

INGREDIENTS

2 pints fresh, ripe strawberries,
   cleaned, hulled, and sliced
2 tablespoons granulated sugar
1 tablespoon cornstarch

1 teaspoon lemon zest
1½ cups heavy cream, whipped
16 crepes (see next page ↗)

METHOD

1. Prepare crepes and set aside
   (see next page ↗).

2. Add half of the sliced
   strawberries to a small
   saucepan and sprinkle with
   sugar. Using a fork, mash
   strawberries to a course puree.

3. Stir in cornstarch and place
   saucepan over medium heat.
   Bring sauce to a boil and stir
   until thickened. Stir in lemon
   zest.

4. Remove from heat, transfer into
   a bowl, and chill in the
   refrigerator.

5. Once strawberry puree is
   chilled, fold in the whipped
   cream.

6. To assemble crepes, place a
   large spoonful of sliced
   strawberries down the center of
   the crepe. Top with several
   dollops of the strawberry cream
   filling and roll up the crepes.
   Repeat process until all crepes
   are assembled.

7. Place two crepes on each plate
   and garnish with slices of fresh
   strawberries. Sprinkle each
   serving generously with
   powdered sugar. ✖

BASIC CREPE BATTER
Makes about 16 crepes

INGREDIENTS

1½ cups milk
¾ cup all-purpose flour
2 eggs
¼ teaspoon salt
1 tablespoon butter, melted

METHOD

1. Place all ingredients in a blender or food processor and combine until smooth. Pour into a large pitcher to facilitate portioning.

2. Lightly grease an 8-inch, nonstick sauté pan and place over medium heat. Ladle batter into the pan and tilt to distribute batter evenly on the bottom of the pan. Cook the crepe on the first side until the edges look dry, about 45 to 60 seconds. Turn the crepe over and briefly cook the second side, for about 30 more seconds. Remove from pan, and repeat process until batter is gone. ✖

FRITTATA GENOVESE

A frittata is the Italian version of the omelette. Various fillings are mixed in with the eggs, which are usually baked and served open-faced. This preparation is useful if you are serving several people, since one large frittata can be prepared and sliced into portions rather than making individual omelets for everyone.

Yields 4 servings

INGREDIENTS

8 large eggs
3 tablespoons olive oil
1 cup mushrooms, sliced
1 clove garlic, minced
¾ cup scallions, chopped
1 cup smoked ham, diced

4 artichoke hearts, sliced
½ cup roasted red pepper, diced
¼ cup fresh basil, chopped
¼ cup fresh parsley, chopped
1 cup fresh Parmesan cheese, grated

METHOD

1. Preheat oven to 350 degrees.

2. Whisk eggs in a large bowl and set aside.

3. Heat olive oil in a large cast-iron or nonstick, ovenproof skillet over medium heat. Add the mushrooms, garlic, and scallions and sauté briefly until tender. Stir in the ham, artichoke hearts, roasted pepper, and fresh basil and parsley.

4. Reduce heat to low and slowly pour eggs into the pan. Sprinkle Parmesan cheese over eggs and let sit on the burner for a minute, without stirring.

5. Place skillet in the oven and bake for 8 to 10 minutes, until eggs are set, being careful not to overcook.

6. Remove from oven. Slice into wedges and serve immediately. ✖

FRUIT SMOOTHIE

This is our favorite morning treat — nature's candy in a glass!

INGREDIENTS

1 banana

10 to 12 strawberries, frozen, with
no sugar added

8 ounces pineapple or orange juice

2 to 4 ice cubes

METHOD

1. Process banana, strawberries, juice, and ice in blender until smooth and thick.

2. Pour into a large glass and serve. ✶

GREAT HOMEFRIES

At Fog Island, we feel that potatoes are an important part
of the morning meal, providing substance and a wholesome,
down-to-earth taste. We take great pride in the potatoes
we serve and are happy to share our recipe.

Yields 6 to 8 servings

INGREDIENTS

2½ to 3 pounds red bliss potatoes, scrubbed
½ cup clarified butter (p. 6)
1 cup onion, diced
½ cup green pepper, diced

½ cup red pepper, diced
1 teaspoon paprika
½ teaspoon chili powder
Salt and black pepper, to taste

METHOD

1. In a large pot, cover potatoes with cold water. Bring to a boil and remove from heat when they are cooked but still firm. Pour into a colander and drain well. Place on a sheetpan to cool.

2. Dice cooked potatoes, leaving the skins on, and set aside.

3. In a large sauté pan, heat 2 tablespoons of clarified butter and add onions and peppers. Cook over medium heat until the vegetables are tender. Remove from heat.

4. Heat a griddle or large nonstick skillet over high heat and add the remaining clarified butter. Add diced potatoes and sprinkle evenly with paprika, chili powder, salt, and black pepper. Cook over medium heat, turning the potatoes occasionally as they become golden brown.

5. Once the potatoes are crispy and evenly browned, add the precooked onion and pepper mixture and toss until hot. Serve immediately. ✖

VARIATIONS

Ultimate Homefries

Place cooked homefries on a sheetpan and top with cooked crumbled bacon and grated cheddar cheese. Place in 400 degree oven and bake for 5 minutes, until cheese is melted. Serve with a dollop of sour cream and sprinkle with finely chopped scallions.

Veggie Homefries

Place cooked homefries on a sheetpan and top with steamed broccoli, sautéed mushrooms and zucchini, diced tomatoes, and grated cheddar. Bake in 400 degree oven to melt the cheese.

HUEVOS RANCHEROS

This is our version of the popular Mexican dish, which in Spanish simply means "country-style eggs." The dried ancho chilies make a delicious sauce, which can be used in many other dishes as well. This ranchero sauce makes a great base sauce for the shredded meat filling in tacos and enchiladas.

Yields 6 servings

INGREDIENTS

1½ to 2 cups ranchero sauce (see next page ↗)
6 large flour tortillas
2 tablespoons clarified butter (p. 6)
12 eggs, fresh
8 ounces Cheddar or Monterey Jack cheese, grated
½ cup scallions, finely chopped
½ cup sour cream
¾ cup guacamole (p. 6)
6 cups Spicy Black Beans (p. 82)
Six sprigs of fresh cilantro, for garnish

METHOD

1. Prepare ranchero sauce in advance (see next page ↗). Warm ranchero sauce in saucepan over low heat.

2. Heat the black beans over low heat and keep warm until ready to serve.

3. On a griddle or in a large sauté pan, cook each tortilla over medium heat until soft, but do not brown. Place each tortilla on an individual serving plate.

4. In a large sauté pan, heat clarified butter and cook eggs over low heat until the whites become opaque. Turn the eggs carefully with a spatula, and cook the tops for a few seconds. Carefully place 2 eggs on top of each heated tortilla.

5. Ladle 4 to 6 tablespoons of the warm ranchero sauce over the eggs and sprinkle with grated cheese. Place under broiler until cheese is melted.

6. Place a serving of black beans on each plate, a dollop of sour cream and guacamole next to the eggs, and sprinkle with chopped scallions. Garnish with fresh cilantro and serve immediately. ✖

RANCHERO SAUCE

This recipe yields more than the amount required for 6 portions of huevos rancheros. Preparing this authentic chili sauce is somewhat time consuming, so at Fog Island we always make large batches. This sauce freezes beautifully.

Yields 6 cups

INGREDIENTS

4 ounces dried ancho chili peppers
(4 to 6 medium-sized chilies)
1 tablespoon vegetable oil
1 large onion, diced
1 tablespoon garlic, minced
1 quart water
1 quart tomato puree
1 tablespoon ground cumin
1 tablespoon fresh cilantro, chopped
2 teaspoons salt
1 tablespoon chili powder
1 tablespoon granulated sugar
1 teaspoon Fog Island Real Hot Sauce (or to taste)

METHOD

1. Clean chili peppers, removing stems and seeds. Use caution when cleaning chilies, being careful not to rub your eyes or nose or you will get a painful stinging sensation.

2. Heat vegetable oil in a saucepot, add onions and garlic and cook over low heat until translucent.

3. Add chilies and water to the pot and bring to a boil. Reduce heat and simmer uncovered for 25 to 30 minutes.

4. Remove pot from heat and let cool. In a blender, puree the chilies with the cooking liquid until very smooth. Return the pureed chili mixture to the saucepot and place back on the burner.

5. Stir in tomato puree and all the seasonings. Simmer uncovered for 20 to 30 minutes, until the sauce thickens slightly and the flavors are enhanced.

6. Taste the sauce and adjust seasoning to desired spiciness. ✄

MEXICAN CORN CAKES

These savory pancakes are a great brunch item and one of our menu favorites among the Fog Island chefs.

Yields about 12 pancakes

INGREDIENTS

½ cup all-purpose flour
¼ cup yellow cornmeal
½ teaspoon salt
1 teaspoon baking soda
1½ teaspoons sugar
¼ teaspoon ground cumin
Dash of Fog Island Real Hot Sauce, to taste
1 egg
½ cup milk

½ cup sour cream
3 tablespoons butter, melted
½ cup corn kernels (frozen or fresh)
¼ cup red pepper, diced and cooked
1 tablespoon scallions or chives, finely chopped
Garnish with sour cream, salsa, and chopped scallions

METHOD

1. In a large bowl, mix flour, cornmeal, salt, baking soda, sugar, cumin, and cayenne pepper until well blended.

2. Add egg, milk, sour cream, and melted butter and stir until the dry ingredients are moistened. Be careful not to overmix; small lumps are fine.

3. Fold in corn, red pepper, and scallions just until mixed.

4. Heat a skillet or griddle to medium hot and grease lightly. Spoon out about 4 tablespoons of batter per corn cake and cook until a few bubbles break on top.

5. Flip cakes and cook other side. Remove from griddle. Garnish with a dollop of sour cream and tomato salsa and sprinkle with finely chopped scallions. Serve immediately. ✛

Morning Crunch Granola

Low in fat . . . high in crunch! We recommend serving this with lowfat vanilla yogurt and fresh berries.

Yields about 12 servings

INGREDIENTS

1 pound rolled oats
4 ounces sliced almonds
4 ounces walnut pieces
1 cup unsweetened shredded
   coconut
1½ teaspoons ground cinnamon

1 orange, zested
3 ounces honey
3 ounces pure maple syrup
1 cup apple juice
4 ounces raisins

METHOD

1. Mix together rolled oats, nuts, coconut, cinnamon, and orange zest in a large bowl.

2. Stir in honey, maple syrup, and apple juice and combine well.

3. Spread onto a sheetpan and distribute evenly.

4. Bake mixture in a 325 degree oven for about 10 minutes, until the top layer begins to turn golden brown.

5. Remove mixture from oven and stir to ensure the granola browns evenly. Return mixture to oven.

6. Repeat this process until the granola is evenly browned and somewhat crispy. Remove from oven and let cool.

7. Add raisins and stir to distribute. Store in an airtight container, so the granola stays crunchy and fresh. ✄

SUGGESTION
Dried Fruits
   Try adding other dried fruits such as apricots, pineapple or dates.

Morning Fog Oatmeal

Oats make a wonderfully filling hot breakfast cereal. In this country, most of the oats available in grocery stores are rolled oats, which are steamed and rolled into flakes. The difference between regular and quick-cooking oats is simply the thickness of the oat flake which affects the cooking time needed.

Yields 4 servings

INGREDIENTS

3 cups water or milk
1⅓ cups rolled oats
½ teaspoon salt
½ teaspoon ground cinnamon

1 tablespoon honey
1 teaspoon orange zest
2 ounces dried cranberries (or raisins)

METHOD

1. Bring water or milk to a boil and gradually add oats in a thin stream, stirring constantly.

2. Reduce heat and simmer uncovered for 7 to 10 minutes, stirring often.

3. Add salt, cinnamon, honey, orange zest, and dried cranberries and stir to incorporate. Remove from heat, cover the pot, and let stand before serving for another 3 to 5 minutes. ✼

OMELETTES

There are a number of ways to prepare an omelette and, in general, most people have very defined personal preferences. At Fog Island we serve three-egg omelettes cooked in the French style: firm on the outside and soft on the inside.

Yields 1 serving

INGREDIENTS

3 eggs
1 to 2 teaspoons clarified butter (p. 6)

½ cup desired filling (suggestions on next page ↗)

METHOD

1. Crack eggs in a small bowl and beat well.

2. Place an 8-inch sauté pan, preferably with a nonstick surface, over medium-high heat and add clarified butter. When butter is fairly hot (don't let it burn), pour in eggs. Immediately begin stirring eggs with a rubber spatula in a circular motion until the eggs begin to set. Using the spatula, evenly distribute eggs in the pan. Let sit undisturbed for about 10 seconds until the top looks almost fully set but still slightly moist.

3. Spread your filling evenly across the center of the omelette, perpendicular to the handle of the pan. If you are adding cheese, sprinkle it on top of the filling.

4. Place omelette under the broiler for a minute or so to melt the cheese. Using the rubber spatula, fold the omelette in half. Invert and slide the omelette onto a warmed serving plate. ✖

SUGGESTED OMELETTE FILLINGS

Apple and Brie

*Sausage, tri-colored peppers, and
   Mozzarella*

Cream cheese and chives

Asparagus and Cheddar

*Spinach and mushroom with Swiss
   cheese*

Brie and sun-dried tomatoes

*Bacon, tomato, onion, and
   Mozzarella*

*Broccoli, mushroom, tomato, and
   scallion*

*Smoked salmon with cream cheese
   and fresh dill*

Fresh herbs and Cheddar

*Avocado, tomato, scallions, and
   Monterey Jack*

Sour cream and caviar

PESTO SCRAMBLED EGGS

If you are not an egg afficionado, take heart. There are many variations of scrambled eggs that make eating eggs exciting!

Yields 6 servings

INGREDIENTS

2 tablespoons clarified butter (p. 6)

12 eggs

6 tablespoons pesto (see next page ➚)

¾ cup spinach, cooked

6 ounces grated Cheddar cheese

METHOD

1. Crack eggs into a bowl and whisk until fully mixed.

2. Heat clarified butter in a large sauté pan, preferably with a nonstick surface, over low heat. Pour in eggs and add pesto, spinach, and cheese. Gently stir eggs with a rubber spatula, scraping the bottom and sides of the pan. Continue to cook until eggs reach desired consistency.

3. Portion onto warmed plates and serve immediately with Great Homefries (p. 17) or Spicy Black Beans (p. 82). ✖

BASIL PESTO

INGREDIENTS

1 clove garlic
¼ teaspoon salt
1½ cups basil leaves, packed
1 tablespoon pine nuts
¼ cup olive oil
¼ cup grated Parmesan cheese

METHOD

1. In a food processor, blend garlic, basil, salt, and pine nuts.

2. Slowly add olive oil and process to desired consistency.

3. Add grated Parmesan and blend until smooth.

4. Taste and adjust seasoning as needed. ✖

EGG SCRAMBLE VARIATIONS

Here are a few simple ideas—
the possibilities are really unlimited:

Fresh herbs and cream cheese

Brie and sun-dried tomatoes

Bacon, onions, and diced tomatoes

Salsa and sour cream

Mushrooms and fresh thyme

Avocado, scallions, red pepper, and Monterey Jack

Western-style with ham, onions, peppers, and Cheddar

Broccoli and Cheddar

Curried vegetables

Sweet Italian sausage with peppers, onions, and mozzarella

POTATO PANCAKES

Unlike many potato pancake recipes, these potato pancakes start with raw potatoes and produce a crisp, golden brown pancake. Delicious served with sour cream and warmed cinnamon applesauce.

Yields 12 to 16 pancakes

INGREDIENTS

4 medium potatoes, peeled and grated (to make 4 cups)
2 eggs
½ cup heavy cream
¼ cup all-purpose flour

Salt and black pepper, to taste
¼ cup clarified butter (p. 6)
Sour cream
Warmed cinnamon applesauce
(see next page ⤴)

METHOD

1. Grate potatoes and keep in cold water to prevent discoloring. When ready to use, drain very well and place in a large bowl.

2. Add eggs, heavy cream, and flour and stir well to incorporate. Season with salt and lots of ground black pepper.

3. Place a large skillet over medium-high heat and add clarified butter. Measure about ¼ cup of potato batter and drop into the hot skillet. Flatten the mound of potato with a spatula. Continue to spoon pancakes into the skillet, being careful not to overcrowd.

4. Cook until edges are golden brown. Then turn with spatula and cook other side for an equivalent amount of time. Remove from pan and pat on paper towels to absorb excess butter. Store in a warm oven until all the pancakes are cooked.

5. Serve with a dollop of sour cream and warmed cinnamon applesauce (see next page ⤴). ✖

CINNAMON APPLESAUCE

INGREDIENTS

4 Granny Smith apples, peeled,
   cored, and sliced
½ cup water
2 to 3 tablespoons sugar
1 teaspoon ground cinnamon
¼ teaspoon ground nutmeg
1 tablespoon lemon juice

METHOD

1. Add apples and water to a
   saucepan. Cook uncovered over
   medium heat, stirring often,
   until apples become soft.
2. Add sugar, cinnamon, nutmeg,
   and lemon juice. Stir to blend
   well. Cook for several more
   minutes to blend flavors.

3. Remove from heat and mash
   apples with a fork to desired
   consistency. ✖

ZESTY LEMON PANCAKES WITH RASPBERRY SAUCE

In the summertime, these light, lemony pancakes make an excellent Sunday morning special.

Yields 4 to 6 servings

INGREDIENTS

4 eggs, separated
¼ cup granulated sugar
¼ cup milk
½ cup sour cream
¼ cup lemon juice
1 tablespoon grated lemon zest
1½ cups all-purpose flour

1 teaspoon baking soda
¼ teaspoon salt
2 tablespoons melted butter
Sprigs of fresh mint, for garnish
Red raspberry sauce (see next page ↗)

METHOD

1. In a mixing bowl beat egg yolks with half the sugar for several minutes, until they begin to thicken.

2. Whisk milk, sour cream, lemon juice, and lemon zest into this bowl with the thickened egg yolks. Stir well to incorporate.

3. In another large bowl, mix together flour, baking soda, and salt.

4. Pour in egg mixture and melted butter. Stir until smooth, being careful not to overmix.

5. In a clean bowl, beat egg whites with the remaining sugar until they hold soft peaks. Fold egg whites gently into pancake batter.

6. Heat a skillet or griddle over medium heat. Grease lightly and ladle batter into skillet. Cook each pancake for about 1½ minutes. Flip pancake over and cook for another minute or so.

7. Place several pancakes on each serving plate and sprinkle generously with powdered sugar. Gently spoon the raspberry sauce (see next page ↗) over the pancakes and garnish with a sprig of fresh mint. ✄

RED RASPBERRY SAUCE

This sauce is incredibly simple to make.

Yields 1½ cups

INGREDIENTS

4 cups raspberries, fresh or frozen
½ cup granulated sugar (or to
    taste, depending on the
    sweetness of the fruit)
2 tablespoons frozen lime juice
    concentrate, thawed

METHOD

1. Place raspberries, sugar, and
   lime juice in a saucepan and
   cook over low heat, stirring
   frequently. Continue to cook
   until berries soften and the
   sauce begins to thicken, about
   15 to 20 minutes. Taste for
   sweetness and add sugar as
   needed.

2. Remove from heat and strain
   sauce through a fine mesh
   strainer. Refrigerate until ready
   to use. ✳

II
BAKED FRESH DAILY

The aromas of freshly baked cinnamon buns or
giant chocolate chunk cookies hot from the oven
are irresistible any time of day.

We are excited to have our own on-premise bakery, where we
prepare the pastries, breads, and desserts served at the Cafe.

Our baked goods are proudly made from "scratch" using the
highest quality ingredients available.

Apple Raspberry Buckle

A buckle is a country-style coffee cake that takes advantage of the abundant fruit harvests in the summertime. Any fresh fruit that suits your fancy may be used. Simply spread the fruit on the bottom of a cake pan, pour over this sweet cake batter and finish with the crumb topping.

Yields one cake (9 x 9-inch pan)

INGREDIENTS

BATTER
¼ cup butter
¾ cup sugar
1 egg
1 teaspoon vanilla
2 cups all-purpose flour
2½ teaspoons baking powder
½ teaspoon salt
½ cup milk

1 cup apples, peeled, cored, and diced
1 cup red raspberries, fresh or frozen

TOPPING
¼ cup sugar
¼ cup all-purpose flour
1 teaspoon ground cinnamon
¼ cup butter, softened

METHOD

1. Preheat oven to 375 degrees and grease cake pan.

2. In a large mixing bowl, cream butter and sugar until light and fluffy. Add egg and vanilla and mix until well blended.

3. Sift together flour, baking powder, and salt. Alternately add the dry ingredients and milk to the creamed butter mixture. Mix batter until smooth, being careful not to overmix.

4. Blend apples and raspberries and spread over the bottom of the greased cake pan. Pour the batter on top. Use a rubber spatula to spread the batter evenly.

5. For the topping, blend sugar, flour, cinnamon, and butter until they reach crumbly consistency. Sprinkle the crumbs on top of the batter.

6. Place in the oven and bake for about 25 minutes, until fully cooked. ✄

BANANA BREAD

This moist bread is incredibly easy to prepare and a wonderful way to use bananas that are a little past their prime.
We have served Banana Bread French Toast
as a breakfast special on several occasions.

Yields one loaf

INGREDIENTS

¼ cup butter

1 cup brown sugar

1 egg

2 large, very ripe bananas, mashed

1½ cups all-purpose flour

2½ teaspoons baking soda

1 teaspoon salt

½ cup walnuts, chopped

METHOD

1. Preheat oven to 325 degrees and grease loaf pan.

2. Melt butter in a small saucepan and set aside to cool.

3. In a large mixing bowl, beat together brown sugar and egg. Add cooled butter and mashed bananas and mix until incorporated.

4. Stir in the flour, baking soda, salt, and nuts. Mix until the dry ingredients become moist, being careful not to overmix the batter.

5. Pour batter into a greased loaf pan and bake for 50 to 60 minutes, until a toothpick inserted in the center of the bread comes out clean.

6. Remove from oven and allow bread to cool for 10 to 15 minutes before removing from the pan. Serve warm. ✖

BUTTERMILK BISCUITS

At the Cafe we always serve these biscuits with our homemade soups at lunchtime, so we prepare quite a few every day.
They are fairly simple to make and delicious
when served hot out of the oven.

Yields 12 biscuits

INGREDIENTS

3 cups all-purpose flour
3 tablespoons granulated sugar
1½ tablespoons baking powder
1 teaspoon salt
6 ounces unsalted butter

3 eggs
¾ cup buttermilk
Egg wash: whisk together 1 egg,
    1 egg yolk, and 1 tablespoon
    water

METHOD

1. Preheat oven to 350 degrees and lightly grease a sheetpan.

2. Measure flour, sugar, baking powder, and salt and combine in a large mixing bowl. Chop butter into small pieces and cut into dry ingredients, working the large clumps with your hands.

3. Add eggs and buttermilk. Mix until dry ingredients become moistened and the dough just begins to come together. Do not overmix or the biscuits will not have a light, tender texture.

4. On a lightly floured surface, roll out dough to ½-inch thickness.

Cut biscuits with a 2½-inch round cutter and place on sheetpan. Reroll dough as needed until all the biscuits are formed.

5. Make an egg wash by whisking together the egg and egg yolk with the water in a small bowl. Brush each biscuit lightly with egg wash and place in preheated oven.

6. Bake 10 to 15 minutes, until lightly golden. Remove from oven and serve warm with Fog Island Nantucket Red Raspberry Preserves or Fog Island Orange Marmalade. ✄

CINNAMON SWIRL COFFEE CAKE

very good This makes a moist, rich cake that is very popular with our
morning take-out coffee customers.

Yields 1 cake

INGREDIENTS

FILLING

½ cup light brown sugar
2 teaspoons ground cinnamon
1 teaspoon cocoa powder
⅔ cup walnuts, chopped
or pecans

added ¼ tsp espresso powder

BATTER

½ cup butter
1 cup granulated sugar
2 eggs
1½ teaspoons vanilla
2 cups all-purpose flour
¼ teaspoon salt
1 teaspoon baking powder
1 teaspoon baking soda
1⅓ cups sour cream *or plain yogurt*

METHOD

1. Preheat oven to 350 degrees and ~~grease loaf~~ pan.

2. In a small bowl, add the brown sugar, cinnamon, cocoa powder, and walnuts for the coffee cake filling and mix well. Set aside for later use.

3. To make the batter, add butter and sugar to a large mixing bowl and cream together until smooth. Add eggs and vanilla and continue to beat well until light and creamy.

4. Sift flour, salt, baking powder, and baking soda together in a separate bowl.

5. Slowly add dry ingredients and sour cream to the batter in stages, alternating between the two and mixing well after each addition. Continue to beat until the batter is smooth.

6. With a rubber spatula, spread half the batter into the greased loaf pan. Sprinkle half the filling on top of the batter in the pan. Top with remaining batter and spread evenly with spatula.

7. With a small paring knife, swirl the batter in circular patterns to create a marbled effect. Sprinkle remaining filling on top of the ⟩

coffee cake and shake pan to distribute evenly.

8. Bake for 40 to 45 minutes, until a toothpick inserted into the center of the cake comes out clean.

9. Remove from oven and let rest 5 to 10 minutes in the pan. Invert onto a rack and cool a little longer before slicing. Serve warm. ✖

needs much larger pan and longer cooking time – 50 mins?

Bundt pan – perfect – bake about 40 mins – test

Country Grain Bread

If you are making a picnic lunch, you can't beat sandwiches made on this wholesome country loaf.

Yields one large loaf

INGREDIENTS

1½ tablespoons or packages active dry yeast

1¾ cups lukewarm water

2 tablespoons vegetable oil

2 tablespoons molasses

1 tablespoon honey

2 cups all-purpose flour

2 cups whole wheat flour

1 teaspoon salt

½ cup unprocessed bran

½ cup rolled oats

Egg wash: whisk together 1 egg, 1 egg yolk, and 1 tablespoon water

---

METHOD

1. Dissolve yeast in lukewarm water and let sit for several minutes.

2. Add remaining ingredients except rolled oats and knead bread dough until smooth and elastic. If the dough is too soft, add additional all-purpose flour to make it more manageable.

3. Place the dough in a greased bowl. Cover and let rise in a warm spot for an hour or so, until doubled in size. Punch the dough down.

4. On a lightly floured surface, roll dough into a smooth round ball. Cover and let rise for 20 to 30 minutes longer. Shape the dough and place into greased 8½ x 4½

x 3-inch loaf pans. Loosely cover and let the dough rise over the top of the loaf pan.

5. Preheat oven to 350 degrees as the dough is in the final rising stage. Brush each loaf with egg wash and score several slash marks with a serrated knife. Sprinkle with rolled oats to garnish.

6. Bake for about 45 minutes. To test for doneness, when the loaf has reached a golden-brown color, carefully remove from loaf pan and tap gently with your fingertips. The tapping should produce a hollow sound. When done, remove from oven and turn onto a rack to cool. Slice when cooled. ✖

CRANBERRY OATMEAL COOKIES

The addition of cranberries and orange zest gives
this chewy traditional cookie a local flair.
Cranberries are plentiful on Nantucket, which is home
to the world's largest natural cranberry bog.

Yields 3 dozen cookies

INGREDIENTS

1 pound butter
1½ cups brown sugar
¾ cup granulated sugar
3 eggs
1 teaspoon vanilla
2 cups rolled oats
2¼ cups all-purpose flour

2 teaspoons baking soda
1 teaspoon salt
1½ teaspoons ground cinnamon
1 tablespoon orange zest
2 cups shredded coconut
2 cups sliced cranberries (frozen
or dried)

METHOD

1. Preheat oven to 350 degrees and grease the cookie sheets.

2. In a large mixing bowl, cream butter and sugars together until smooth and fluffy. Beat in eggs and vanilla and mix well.

3. Add oats, flour, baking soda, salt, and cinnamon to the butter mixture and mix thoroughly.

4. Stir in orange zest, shredded coconut, and dried cranberries and mix until evenly distributed in the dough.

5. Drop cookies by rounded tablespoonsful onto greased cookie sheet, spacing 2 inches apart.

6. Bake for 12 to 14 minutes, until the cookies are golden brown.

7. Remove the cookies from the oven and wait a few minutes before transferring to cooling racks. These cookies are somewhat fragile until they cool. ✄

FRENCH BAGUETTE

For your French bread to have an authentic crispy crust,
you will need steam during the baking process. If you do
not have the luxury of a steam-injected oven, simply place
a roasting pan filled with a $^1/_2$ inch of boiling water in the
bottom of the oven. Another option is to occasionally
spritz the baguettes with water as the loaves are baking.

Yields 2 long baguettes (24-inch pans)

INGREDIENTS

2 cups lukewarm water
1 tablespoon or 1 package active
  dry yeast
3¾ to 4 cups all-purpose flour
3¾ to 4 cups bread flour (high-
  gluten)

1 tablespoon salt
Egg wash: whisk together 1 egg,
  1 egg yolk, and 1 tablespoon
  water

METHOD

1. Dissolve yeast in lukewarm
   water and let sit for several
   minutes.

2. Add flour and salt and knead the
   bread dough until smooth and
   elastic. If the dough is too soft,
   add additional all-purpose flour to
   make a more manageable dough.

3. Place the dough in a clean bowl.
   Cover and let rise in a warm
   spot for an hour or so, until
   double in size. Punch down the
   dough.

4. On a lightly floured surface,
   divide the dough and roll into
   two smooth, round balls. Cover

and let rise for about 20 minutes
longer for the gluten to relax.

5. Using the palms of your hands,
   shape the dough into rectangles,
   pushing down to eliminate air
   pockets. Roll the dough tightly
   into a cylinder shape, keeping
   the ends even. Press outward
   with your hands and taper the
   dough toward the ends until
   long baguette shapes are
   formed. The shaped dough at
   this point should be the length
   of the baguette pans. Place the
   baguettes, seam side down,
   in the greased pans, cover, and
   set in a warm place to rise. ➚

6. Let dough rise until somewhat less than double in size, about 30 to 40 minutes. As the dough is rising, spritz with water every 15 minutes or so to keep moist.

7. Preheat oven to 375 degrees when the bread is in the final rising stage. Brush egg wash on the tops of each baguette with a pastry brush. Score several slash marks with a serrated knife and let baguettes cor to rest for another 10 to 1 minutes.

8. Place bread in preheated ove. and bake for about 35 to 45 minutes, until evenly brown. After taking the baguettes out of the oven, immediately remove the loaves from the pans and place on a cooling rack. ✶

GIANT CHOCOLATE CHUNK COOKIES

We usually feature these oversized cookies around the
holidays. The absence of eggs results in a buttery shortbread
consistency which is rather different than our traditional
chocolatte chip cookie..

Yields about 18 giant cookies

INGREDIENTS

1 pound butter

2 cups granulated sugar

1 tablespoon vanilla

1 teaspoon salt

4 cups all-purpose flour

1 teaspoon baking soda

2 cups walnuts, chopped

1 pound semisweet chocolate
    chunks, cut into smaller chunks

METHOD

1. Preheat oven to 350 degrees and lightly grease cookie sheet.

2. Cream together butter and sugar until light and creamy. Add vanilla and salt and blend until incorporated.

3. Add flour and baking soda and continue to mix until a smooth dough is formed.

4. Stir in chopped walnuts and chocolate chunks and mix until evenly distributed.

5. Scoop cookie dough using a large scoop, about 4 ounces, and place on greased cookie sheet. Flatten each cookie to ½-inch thickness using a rubber spatula.

6. Bake in preheated oven for about 15 minutes, until golden brown. Remove from oven and allow to cool before moving from cookie sheet. �֎

GINGER CREAM SCONES

Scones are simply sweetened biscuits; they stay fresher longer than regular biscuits because of a higher proportion of fat and sugar. This basic recipe can be used to create different flavors by adding variations of spices, dried and fresh fruits, or by substituting different grains such as oats or bran for some of the flour.

Yields 12 scones

INGREDIENTS

2¼ cups all-purpose flour
1 tablespoon baking powder
¼ cup sugar
½ teaspoon salt
1 teaspoon ground ginger

2 tablespoons crystallized ginger, finely diced
1¼ cups heavy cream
2 tablespoons butter, melted
2 tablespoons granulated sugar

METHOD

1. Preheat oven to 400 degrees.

2. In a large mixing bowl, combine flour, baking powder, sugar, salt, and both ground and crystallized ginger.

3. In a separate bowl whip the heavy cream until it forms soft peaks.

4. Add cream to the dry ingredients and fold until the dough holds together, being careful not to overmix.

5. Place dough on a lightly floured surface and roll into circular shape about 10 inches in diameter. Using a pastry brush, spread butter evenly over the top of the dough, then sprinkle evenly with sugar. Cut the circle into 12 even wedges and place pieces on an ungreased baking sheet spacing at least an inch apart.

6. Bake in preheated oven for about 15 minutes, until golden brown. Remove from oven and serve warm. ✖

GINGERSNAP COOKIES

A hint of ground black pepper adds spiciness to the ginger
flavor of these old-fashioned, buttery cookies.

Yields 3 dozen cookies

INGREDIENTS

¾ cup butter

1 cup brown sugar

1 egg

¼ cup molasses

2¼ cups all-purpose flour

2 teaspoons baking soda

½ teaspoon salt

1 teaspoon ground cinnamon

1 teaspoon ground ginger

1 teaspoon allspice

½ teaspoon ground black pepper

½ teaspoon ground nutmeg

METHOD

1. Preheat oven to 375 degrees and grease the cookie sheets.

2. In a large mixing bowl, cream butter and brown sugar together until smooth and fluffy. Beat in egg and then molasses.

3. Sift together flour, baking soda, salt, and spices. Add dry ingredients to the creamed butter mixture and mix thoroughly.

4. Shape dough into 1½ inch balls and place at least 2 inches apart on greased cookie sheets.

5. Bake for 15 minutes, until almost firm to the touch.

6. Remove from oven and sprinkle evenly with granulated sugar. ✖

GLAZED CINNAMON BUNS

Rolling cinnamon sugar and raisins into croissant dough makes these breakfast buns exceptionally flaky and buttery.

Yields 16 buns

INGREDIENTS

1 tablespoon or 1 package active
   dry yeast
½ cup water, lukewarm
1½ cups milk
¼ cup sugar
1½ teaspoons salt
4½ to 5 cups all-purpose flour
1 pound unsalted butter, room
   temperature

FILLING

½ cup cinnamon sugar (½ cup
   sugar plus 2 teaspoons
   cinnamon)
½ cup raisins

GLAZE

1 cup confectioners' sugar
1 tablespoon milk

METHOD

1. Dissolve yeast in the water and let sit for several minutes.

2. Add milk, sugar, salt, and flour and knead dough just until the dough forms together. If the dough is overmixed, the gluten in the flour will make the dough much more difficult to roll out, resulting in a less flaky pastry.

3. In a separate mixing bowl, whip butter until smooth and set aside.

4. Place dough on a liberally floured surface and, using a rolling pin, roll out into a rectangular shape with ½-inch thickness. Brush off excess flour with a dry pastry brush.

5. Take all the softened butter from the mixing bowl and smear evenly over half the rolled-out dough, leaving an inch border around the sides. Fold dough in half to lock in the butter.

6. Rotate the dough 90 degrees and liberally spread flour under the dough to eliminate sticking during the rolling process. Roll out the dough again into a rectangle shape slightly larger than the first time. Brush off excess flour and, this time, fold the rectangle into thirds. ⌇

7. Rotate the dough again and repeat this rolling process two more times, folding dough in thirds each time. If the dough becomes difficult to roll or the butter inside begins to leak out when rolling, place on a floured sheetpan and refrigerate 15 to 20 minutes. This will firm up the butter and make the dough easier to work with.

8. After the dough has been given 3 three-folds, refrigerate for several hours, preferably overnight, before rolling out dough a last time.

9. After the dough has relaxed completely, place on a lightly floured surface, and roll out into a rectangular shape about $\frac{1}{4}$ inch thick.

10. Sprinkle evenly with cinnamon sugar, being careful to leave an inch border on the bottom of the rectangle. Distribute raisins evenly over the dough.

11. Roll the rectangle tightly from top to bottom, making sure the sides are even. Pinch seam together tightly with fingers. Cut the cylinder of dough evenly into $1\frac{1}{2}$-inch circles.

12. Space each cinnamon roll an inch or so apart on a lightly greased sheetpan. Let cinnamon rolls rise in a warm spot for 30 minutes, until puffy to the touch. Preheat oven to 350 degrees.

13. Place rolls in oven and bake for 20 minutes, until golden brown. Remove from oven and let cool slightly.

14. To make the glaze, combine the confectioners' sugar and milk in a small bowl. Drizzle cinnamon buns with the glaze. Serve warm whenever possible. ✖

HEALTH NUT MUFFINS

These muffins have been described as a cross between zucchini bread and carrot cake. The addition of applesauce and crushed pineapple makes these muffins extremely moist.

Yields 14 to 16 muffins

INGREDIENTS

2¼ cups all-purpose flour
1 cup light brown sugar
2 teaspoons baking soda
2 teaspoons ground cinnamon
½ teaspoon ground ginger
½ teaspoon ground nutmeg
½ teaspoon salt
3 eggs
¾ cup vegetable oil

½ cup shredded coconut
1 cup carrots, grated
1 cup zucchini, grated
¾ cup applesauce (p. 29)
1 cup pineapple, crushed and drained
½ cup dried cranberries
½ cup walnuts, chopped

METHOD

1. Preheat oven to 350 degrees.

2. In a large mixing bowl, mix together flour, brown sugar, baking soda, cinnamon, ginger, nutmeg, and salt.

3. Add eggs and vegetable oil to the dry ingredients and mix until incorporated. Stir in coconut, carrots, zucchini, applesauce, pineapple, cranberries, and walnuts until evenly distributed, being careful not to overmix.

4. Lightly grease muffin tins or line with paper liners. Scoop batter into the muffin tins, filling each one all the way to the top.

5. Bake in preheated oven for 35 to 40 minutes, until golden brown and thoroughly cooked in the middle (until a toothpick comes out clean when inserted in the center).

6. Remove muffins from oven and cool in pans for at least 10 to 15 minutes, then turn out onto cooling rack. ✄

LEMON POPPY SEED COFFEE CAKE

Grating and juicing the lemons and oranges for this recipe
is somewhat tedious, but well worth the effort once you taste
the finished product.

Yields one Bundt cake

INGREDIENTS

½ cup poppy seeds
¼ cup water
1½ cups butter
1½ cups granulated sugar
2 tablespoons lemon zest
1 tablespoon orange zest
8 eggs, separated

2 cups all-purpose flour
½ teaspoon salt

SOAKING LIQUID

¼ cup lemon juice
1 tablespoon orange juice
2 tablespoons granulated sugar

METHOD

1. Place poppy seeds and water in a small bowl and soak for 30 minutes. Drain poppy seeds and set aside.

2. Preheat oven to 350 degrees and liberally grease a 10-inch bundt pan (or 10-inch cake pan).

3. In a large mixing bowl, cream butter and half the sugar until light and fluffy. Slowly add egg yolks and beat until smooth. Add lemon zest, orange zest, and poppy seeds and mix until well blended.

4. Sift together the flour and salt and add to the batter. Mix on medium speed until fully incorporated.

5. In a separate bowl, whip egg whites on high speed until they become frothy. Slowly add the remainder of the sugar and beat egg whites to a stiff peak. Gently fold egg whites into the batter.

6. Pour the batter into the cake pan and distribute evenly.

7. Bake in preheated oven for 35 to 45 minutes, until a toothpick comes out clean when inserted. Remove from oven.

8. To make soaking liquid, combine lemon and orange juices with sugar in a small saucepan. Heat over low heat until sugar is fully dissolved. ⤴

9. Using the tines of a fork or a toothpick, prick small holes in the coffee cake. Slowly pour the liquid over the cake, letting the juice soak into the cake. When cooled, remove from pan and sprinkle generously with powdered sugar. ✵

Mexican Cornbread

At Fog Island, this spicy cornbread makes an excellent accompaniment to our Huevos Rancheros and Breakfast Burrito. For lunch, we grill slices of cornbread to serve with our Black Beans and Rice.

Yields one loaf

INGREDIENTS

1 cup cornmeal
1 cup all-purpose flour
3 tablespoons granulated sugar
1 tablespoon baking powder
½ teaspoon salt
½ cup sour cream
½ cup milk

1 egg
¼ cup butter, melted
½ cup frozen corn niblets
¼ cup red pepper, diced and cooked
Dash cayenne pepper, to taste

METHOD

1. Preheat oven to 350 degrees and grease loaf pan.

2. In a large bowl, combine cornmeal, flour, sugar, baking powder, and salt. Add sour cream, milk, egg, and melted butter. Stir well to incorporate.

3. Add the corn, red pepper, and cayenne pepper and stir until mixed.

4. Pour batter into loaf pan and use a spatula to spread evenly.

5. Bake in preheated oven for about 25 to 30 minutes, until a toothpick comes out clean when inserted in the center. Remove from oven and serve warm. ✖

MORNING FOG MUFFINS

We use this recipe as the basic muffin batter for almost all
of our muffins at the Cafe, then add different fruits and
spices to create a wide assortment of flavors.

Yields 14 to 16 muffins

INGREDIENTS

3 cups all-purpose flour

1½ cups oat bran or unprocessed
wheat bran

1 teaspoon salt

1½ tablespoons baking powder

1 teaspoon baking soda

½ cup granulated sugar

¾ cup brown sugar

2 eggs

¾ cup vegetable oil or melted
butter

1½ cups buttermilk

1½ to 2 cups fruit, chopped

Spices such as cinnamon or
nutmeg, to taste

METHOD

1. Preheat oven to 350 degrees
and grease muffin tins or line
with paper liners.

2. In a large bowl combine flour,
salt, baking powder and soda,
and sugars and mix together.

3. Add eggs, vegetable oil, and
buttermilk and stir until the dry
ingredients become moist. Be
careful not to stir the batter too
much or the muffins will not be
tender.

4. Gently fold in fruit and spices to
distribute evenly.

5. Spoon into greased muffin tins,
filling each cup to the brim.
Sprinkle each muffin with ½ teaspoon granulated sugar, if
desired. Bake for 20 minutes,
until a toothpick comes out
clean when inserted into the
center.

6. Cool in the muffin pan for 10 to
15 minutes, then remove from
the pan and place on a cooling
rack. ✖

Pear Almond
*1½ cups pears, diced; ½ cup
sliced almonds, toasted;
1 teaspoon almond extract.*

Blueberry Lemon
*2 cups blueberries, fresh or
frozen; zest of 2 lemons.*

Cranberry Lime
*2 cups cranberries, fresh or
frozen; zest of 2 limes or
1 tablespoon frozen lime juice
concentrate.*

Banana Granola
*3 bananas, mashed
(equivalent to 1½ cups); ¾
cup Morning Crunch Granola
(p. 22)*

Strawberry Yogurt
*1½ cups fresh strawberries,
chopped; substitute 1 cup
vanilla yogurt and ½ cup
buttermilk for the 1½ cups
buttermilk.*

Apple Blackberry
*1 cup Granny Smith apples
(peeled and diced); ¾ cup
blackberries, fresh or frozen.*

Raspberry Nectarine
*1¼ cups nectarines, diced;
½ cup red raspberries, fresh
or frozen.* ✂

ONION DILL BREAD

This recipe makes an excellent bread for sandwiches since the texture is soft and rather springy. Consider using this dough for dinner rolls as well.

Yields 2 medium loaves or 2 dozen rolls

INGREDIENTS

2 tablespoons or 2 packages active dry yeast
2 cups lukewarm water
2 tablespoons vegetable oil
1 tablespoon dried dill weed
½ cup onions, finely diced

5½ cups all-purpose flour
2 teaspoons salt
Egg wash: whisk together 1 egg, 1 egg yolk, and 1 tablespoon water

---

METHOD

1. Dissolve yeast in lukewarm water and let sit for several minutes.

2. Add remaining ingredients and knead the bread dough until smooth and elastic. If the dough is too soft, add flour to make a more manageable dough.

3. Place the dough in a greased bowl. Cover and let rise in a warm spot for an hour or so, until doubled in size. Punch the dough down and divide in half.

4. On a lightly floured surface roll dough into smooth round balls. Cover and let rise for about 20 minutes longer to relax the gluten. Shape the dough and place into greased 8½ x 4½ x 3-inch loaf pans. Loosely cover and let dough rise over the top of the pans.

5. Preheat oven to 350 degrees while the dough is in the final rising stage. Brush each loaf with egg wash and make several slash marks across the top of each loaf with a serrated knife.

6. Bake for about 45 minutes, until golden brown. You should be able to hear a hollow sound when gently tapping the pan bottom. Remove loaf from pan and place on cooling rack. Slice when cooled. ✖

OLD-FASHIONED
PEANUT BUTTER COOKIES

We have also included a few variations of this
old-fashioned favorite.

Yields 3 dozen cookies

INGREDIENTS

1 cup butter
1 cup chunky peanut butter
1 cup brown sugar
1 cup granulated sugar
2 eggs

2 teaspoons vanilla extract
3½ cups all-purpose flour
½ teaspoon salt
2 teaspoons baking soda
1 teaspoon baking powder

METHOD

1. Preheat oven to 375 degrees and grease cookie sheets.

2. In a large mixing bowl, cream butter, peanut butter, and sugars together until smooth and fluffy. Beat in eggs and vanilla and blend well.

3. Sift together flour, salt, baking soda, and baking powder. Add to the creamed butter mixture and mix thoroughly until combined.

4. Scoop dough by rounded tea-spoonsful and place at least 2 inches apart on cookie sheet. Press each cookie with the tines of a fork, making a crosshatch design.

5. Bake for 10 to 12 minutes, until golden brown.

6. Remove from oven and place on racks to cool. ✖

VARIATIONS

Peanut Butter Chocolate Chip Cookies
Add 12 ounces semisweet chocolate chips to the batter after Step 3.

Reese's Pieces Cookies
Add 12 ounces of Reese's Pieces to the batter after Step 3.

Peanut Butter Kisses
Bake as directed. Immediately after removing the cookies from the oven, press a chocolate kiss into the center of each cookie.

Peanut Butter and Jelly Cups
Bake as directed. Remove from the oven and while still warm, press the center of each cookie with the back of a teaspoon to make an indentation. Fill with ½ teaspoon of Fog Island Nantucket Red Raspberry Preserves.

PERFECT POPOVERS

Popovers are a quick bread miraculously leavened by eggs and
the incorporation of air, which results in steam when the
popovers are baked. The secret to light and lofty popovers
is to mix the ingredients in a blender at high speed to
incorporate as much air as possible.

Yields about 16, depending on size of muffin tins

INGREDIENTS

3 cups milk

4 eggs

3 tablespoons butter, melted

3 cups all-purpose flour

¼ teaspoon salt

METHOD

1. Preheat oven to 450 degrees
   and grease muffin tins liberally.

2. In a blender, mix milk, eggs, and
   butter until well blended. Add
   flour and salt and continue to
   blend on high speed until the
   ingredients are well
   incorporated and the batter is
   bubbly.

3. Pour batter into muffin tins,
   filling to the top. Place in
   preheated oven and bake for 15
   minutes. Reduce oven
   temperature to 350 degrees, but
   do not open the oven door until
   the last 5 to 10 minutes of
   baking. Continue to bake for 20
   to 25 minutes, until golden
   brown all over. Do not remove
   from oven prematurely or the
   popovers will collapse.

4. Remove from pan and serve
   piping hot with butter and Fog
   Island Nantucket Red Raspberry
   Preserves. ✖

VARIATIONS

Parmesan and Chive Popovers
*Blend 1 cup Parmesan cheese,
½ cup chives, and dash of
cayenne pepper into the batter
when the dry ingredients are
added.*

Orange Oatmeal Popovers
*Coarsely grind ¾ cup of rolled
oats in the blender. Mix with
2¼ cups of all-purpose flour
and substitute for the flour in
the main recipe. Before
pouring the batter into the
muffin tin, put a rounded
teaspoon of Fog Island Orange
Marmalade in the bottom of
each greased muffin cup.*

Pecan Sticky Buns

These rich breakfast rolls are dripping with sweet
caramel topping and loaded with crunchy pecans.
Great for an occasional indulgence.

Yields 12 buns

INGREDIENTS

¼ cup warm water
1 cup milk, warmed
1 tablespoon or 1 package active
 dry yeast
1¼ cup butter, melted
¼ cup granulated sugar
1 teaspoon salt
1 egg
3¼ cups all-purpose flour

½ cup cinnamon sugar (½ cup
 sugar plus 1 tablespoon
 cinnamon)

STICKY GOO
½ cup butter
½ pound dark brown sugar
2 tablespoons water
1½ cups pecan pieces

METHOD

1. Pour the water and warm milk
into a large mixing bowl and stir
in yeast until it dissolves. Let
rest for 5 minutes.

2. Add melted butter, sugar, salt,
and egg and beat until well
blended. Add flour and knead
until the ingredients are totally
incorporated and the dough
becomes smooth.

3. Place dough in a greased bowl
and cover. Let rise in a warm
spot 45 minutes to an hour, until
doubled in size.

4. Punch dough down and roll it
out into a rectangle on a lightly

floured table. Sprinkle evenly
with cinnamon sugar and tightly
roll the rectangle, making a long
tube or cylinder shape. Cut the
dough into 12 pieces, about 1½
inches thick.

5. To make the sticky goo, place
butter, brown sugar, and water
in a saucepan over medium heat
until the sugar is dissolved and
the mixture is well blended.
Remove from heat.

6. Spread pecan pieces evenly on
the bottom of an 8 x 12-inch
baking pan. Pour the sticky goo
on top of the pecans and use ↗

a spatula to coat the nuts with the goo.

7. Place the portioned dough on top of the sticky goo. Let dough rise for 30 to 40 minutes in a warm spot until the dough looks puffy. Preheat oven to 350 degrees at this time.

8. Bake for about 35 to 45 minutes, making sure the dough in the center of each bun is thoroughly baked.

9. Remove from oven and immediately invert onto a baking sheet, using extreme caution because of the hot sugar. Let cool slightly before serving. ✖

III
SAVORY SPECIALTIES

The addition of herbs and spices to a recipe dramatically changes the character and flavor of any dish. With regard to flavor, the process of seasoning is the medium to the artistic or creative side of cooking.

This chapter contains a cross-cultural selection of popular recipes as well as local favorites and purposely uses a wide variety of seasonings.

BAMBOO STEAMED VEGGIES

This is a healthy way to cook vegetables to retain their natural nutrients and eliminate the use of fats in the cooking process. At the Cafe we serve these freshly steamed vegetables in an authentic bamboo steamer with brown rice and an Asian-style dipping sauce.

Yields 2 servings

INGREDIENTS

1 large carrot, peeled and sliced on bias

¼ head broccoli, trim flowerettes

¼ head cauliflower, trim flowerettes

1 small yellow squash, sliced on bias

6 asparagus spears, cut in half

½ cup Asian-style dipping sauce (see next page ↗)

3 cups cooked brown rice

METHOD

1. Arrange vegetables in a bamboo steamer and cover with lid.

2. In a large sauté pan or wok, add just enough water to touch the bottom level of the bamboo steamer. Bring the water to a boil.

3. Place the bamboo steamer in the pan and cook for 8 to 10 minutes, just until the vegetables are tender.

4. Remove from heat and place the bamboo steamer on a large platter. Serve immediately with dipping sauce and cooked rice on the side. ✄

ASIAN-STYLE DIPPING SAUCE

This sauce is also wonderful used as a salad dressing tossed with fresh garden greens
Yields 6 to 8 Servings

INGREDIENTS

⅓ cup rice wine vinegar
1 tablespoon sugar
¼ cup soy sauce
1 teaspoon sesame oil
¼ cup vegetable oil
1 cup Thai Peanut Sauce (p. 84)

METHOD

1. In a large mixing bowl whisk together the rice wine vinegar, sugar, soy sauce, and sesame oil.

2. Add the vegetable oil in a slow stream, whisking continuously to incorporate. Continue to whisk until all the oil has been added.

3. Gradually stir in the peanut sauce and mix until thoroughly combined.

4. Refrigerate until ready to serve. ✖

CAESAR SALAD

This salad dressing keeps over a week in the refrigerator, so if you're a big Caesar salad fan, increase the batch size, and you will be set for every night of the week.

Yields 12 servings

INGREDIENTS

DRESSING
1 tablespoon garlic
2 tablespoons Fog Island Stone Ground Mustard
8 anchovies
2 eggs
2 lemons, juiced
1 teaspoon Worcestershire sauce
2 cups olive oil
½ cup grated Parmesan cheese
1 tablespoon water

SALAD
2 heads romaine, washed and dried using lettuce spinner
1½ cups croutons (p. 117)
½ cup grated Parmesan cheese
1 recipe Caesar dressing

METHOD

1. Place garlic, mustard, and anchovies in a food processor and blend to a smooth paste.

2. Add eggs, lemon juice, and Worcestershire sauce and mix to combine.

3. While the machine is running, slowly add the olive oil and blend until dressing emulsifies and all the oil has been added.

4. Add Parmesan cheese and water and continue to blend until well incorporated. Taste and adjust seasoning as needed. Refrigerate until ready to use.

5. Just before serving salad, tear the romaine leaves and place in a large salad bowl.

6. Add dressing and toss romaine until dressing is evenly distributed. Sprinkle with Parmesan and croutons and toss again.

7. Portion on chilled salad plate and garnish with freshly ground black pepper and a couple of anchovy fillets, if desired. Serve immediately so the lettuce remains crisp! ✖

Char-grilled Chicken Caesar
Marinate boneless chicken breasts in olive oil, garlic, and herbs (rosemary, thyme, and oregano). Grill chicken to order and slice into thin strips after cooking. Arrange on top of salad before serving.

Shrimp Caesar
Peel and devein shrimp. Sauté in olive oil with minced garlic. Remove from pan and place on top of Caesar salad. Serve immediately. ✄

Cajun Shrimp Jambalaya

Just to warn you . . . this recipe is quite spicy!
We suggest decreasing the amount of cayenne
pepper if you are not brave of heart.

Yields 4 servings

INGREDIENTS

3 tablespoons clarified butter (p. 6)
1½ cups onions, diced
1 cup celery, diced
¾ cup green pepper, diced
1½ teaspoons garlic, minced

1½ teaspoons salt
1½ teaspoons cayenne pepper, or
   to taste
1½ teaspoons white pepper
½ teaspoon black pepper
1½ teaspoons basil

½ teaspoon leaf thyme
2 bay leaves

2½ cups crushed tomatoes
½ cup vegetable stock
Dash Fog Island Real Hot Sauce,
   to taste
1½ pounds shrimp, medium-sized
   (24–30 per pound), peeled and
   deveined
½ cup scallions, chopped
4 cups cooked brown rice

METHOD

1. Heat 1 tablespoon of the butter in a large saucepan over medium heat and add onions, celery, peppers, and garlic. Cook vegetables until tender, stirring frequently. Add salt, the peppers, basil, thyme, and bay leaves to the vegetables and sauté for 2 to 3 minutes to extract flavors, stirring constantly.

2. Stir in the tomatoes and vegetable stock. Lower heat and simmer for 30 to 40 minutes, reducing sauce until a bit thickened.

3. Taste and adjust seasonings, adding a dash of hot sauce if desired. Remove bay leaves and keep over low heat.

4. In a sauté pan, heat 2 tablespoons of clarified butter and sauté the shrimp over high heat until thoroughly cooked, about 3 to 5 minutes.

5. Add shrimp to the sauce and bring to a low simmer. To serve, ladle over warm brown rice and garnish with chopped scallions. ✖

CARIBBEAN MEAT PIES

When we were vacationing in Antigua several years ago, we developed a serious meat pie addiction. The local market would have a hot batch ready at 3:30 every afternoon just when the local workers were finishing for the day. Like clockwork, we would leave the beach at 3:15, and run to the store in time to purchase a couple of meat pies, piping hot from the oven. This is our best attempt to duplicate this savory pastry.

Yields 8 servings

INGREDIENTS

PASTRY DOUGH

3 cups all-purpose flour
2 teaspoons salt
2 teaspoons curry powder
2 teaspoons turmeric
1 pound butter
4 egg yolks
½ cup milk, cold

MEAT PIE FILLING

1 pound lean ground beef
½ cup onions, minced
2 tablespoons garlic, minced

¾ cup carrots, shredded
½ cup scallions, sliced
2 teaspoons ground cumin
1 tablespoon chili powder
1 tablespoon dried leaf thyme
1 teaspoon Fog Island Real Hot Sauce, or to taste
Salt and black pepper, to taste
¾ cup vegetable stock
¾ cup bread crumbs, finely ground

Egg wash: whisk together 1 egg, 1 egg yolk, and 1 tablespoon water

METHOD

PASTRY DOUGH

1. Put flour, salt, curry powder, and turmeric in a mixing bowl and stir to blend.

2. Cut butter into small pieces and add to dry ingredients using a pastry cutter. Use the tips of your fingers to break apart large clumps of butter, but do not worry if small pieces of butter are still visible.

3. In a separate bowl, whisk egg yolks with cold milk. Add this ↗

68

liquid to the dry ingredients, stirring until dry ingredients are moistened and the dough can be gathered into a smooth ball. Be careful not to overwork the dough or the crust will not be as flaky after baking.

4. Place dough on a lightly floured surface and divide evenly into 8 pieces. Roll into individual balls and refrigerate for several hours.

FILLING

1. In a large skillet, cook ground beef over medium heat until no longer pink, breaking meat apart with a spoon as it cooks. Remove from heat and drain off any excess fat.

2. Add onions, garlic, carrots, and scallions and cook until the vegetables are tender. Stir in cumin, chili powder, thyme, and hot sauce and cook for several minutes, stirring occasionally to extract flavor from the spices.

3 Add vegetable stock and bread crumbs and continue to simmer for 10 to 15 minutes, until the stock reduces and the filling reaches the consistency of moist bread stuffing. Remove from heat and set aside to cool.

ASSEMBLE AND BAKE

1. Preheat oven to 350 degrees and lightly grease a sheetpan.

2. On a lightly floured surface, roll out the pastry dough into a circular shape with about an $\frac{1}{8}$-inch thickness, working the dough from the center to the outside. Using a pastry wheel, trim edges so the pastry shells are uniform circular shapes.

3. Spoon meat filling on one-half of each pastry shell, leaving a $\frac{1}{2}$-inch border around the outside. Wet the edges with water, and fold the shells in half. With the tines of a fork, press edges firmly together to seal.

4. Brush each meat pie with egg wash with a pastry brush.

3. Place meat pies on the sheetpan and bake for 20 to 25 minutes, until uniformly golden brown. Serve piping hot. ✄

CHINESE CHICKEN SALAD

Mark's mother first introduced us to this unusual salad,
which is not only delicious but also a meal in itself.
This is the Fog Island version of this popular salad.

Yields 4 to 6 servings

INGREDIENTS

3 whole boneless chicken breasts,
trimmed and pounded

MARINADE

2 tablespoons sesame oil
2 tablespoons vegetable oil
¼ cup soy sauce
¼ cup rice wine vinegar
2 teaspoons minced ginger
2 teaspoons minced garlic
Dash Fog Island Real Hot Sauce

SALAD

1 large head red leaf lettuce
½ cup shredded carrots
¼ cup chopped scallions
½ cup chopped, unsalted roasted
peanuts
1 package ramen noodles
1 cup Asian-style dipping sauce
(p. 64)
1 tablespoon toasted sesame
seeds

METHOD

1. To make marinade, whisk together sesame oil, vegetable oil, soy sauce, rice wine vinegar, ginger, garlic, and hot sauce in large bowl and mix until well blended. Set aside.

2. Pour marinade over the chicken breasts and let stand for at least 3 to 4 hours or overnight.

3. Grill the chicken breasts until cooked through. Remove from heat and slice into ½-inch strips and set aside.

4. Tear the lettuce into small pieces and place in large mixing bowl. Add carrots, scallions, and peanuts. Break up ramen noodles, add to salad, and toss lightly.

5. Add the Asian-style dipping sauce and toss until the salad is evenly coated.

6. To serve, arrange salad on chilled plates and top with strips of grilled marinated chicken. Garnish with toasted sesame seeds and serve immediately. ✖

EMMENTALER AND GRUYÈRE CHEESE FONDUE

This unique dish from Switzerland is always a favorite
served as a festive appetizer for a small group or as an
intimate dinner for two. We recommend using a fondue
pot when preparing this recipe, which can easily be
found in almost any kitchen supply store.

Yields 4 servings

INGREDIENTS

1 teaspoon garlic, minced
8 ounces Emmentaler cheese,
   grated
8 ounces Gruyère cheese, grated
1½ tablespoons cornstarch
1 to 1¼ cups dry white wine
1½ to 2 tablespoons kirsch

(cherry-flavored brandy)
Dash Fog Island Real Hot Sauce
Dash nutmeg
6 cups French bread, cubed
2 Granny Smith apples, sliced
2 cups broccoli flowerettes,
   steamed

METHOD

1. Rub the sides of a fondue pot
   with garlic.

2. Place grated cheeses and cornstarch in a small bowl and toss
   until cornstarch is mixed in
   evenly. Set aside.

3. Pour white wine into the fondue
   pot and bring just to the
   simmering point. Do not boil.

4. Gradually add cheese to the
   wine, stirring slowly to melt and
   blend. Let simmer for several
   minutes.

5. Finish by stirring in the kirsch
   and season to taste with

   cayenne and nutmeg. If the
   fondue becomes too thick, stir in
   a splash of white wine.

6. Keep warm over a low flame or
   sterno. Serve with French bread
   cubes, sliced apples, and
   steamed broccoli flowerettes. ✖

A FONDUE CUSTOM
*If a woman loses her bread in a
fondue, she pays with a kiss to the
man on her right. If a man loses,
he buys the next round of drinks.* ✖

GRILLED FLATBREAD
WITH ROASTED GARLIC

If you are a garlic lover, this recipe is for you.

Yields 6 servings

INGREDIENTS

½ tablespoon or ½ package active
   dry yeast
¾ cup water, warm
2 teaspoons honey
¾ cup all-purpose flour

¾ cup semolina flour
¼ teaspoon salt
1 tablespoon olive oil
¼ cup cornmeal

METHOD

1. Dissolve yeast in water, add the honey, and let sit for 5 minutes.

2. Add flour, semolina, salt, and olive oil. Knead until a smooth, elastic dough is formed and the dough pulls away cleanly from the bowl. If the dough is too soft, add flour.

3. On a lightly floured surface, divide the dough into 6 equal pieces and round into balls. Cover and let rise 45 minutes to 1 hour, until doubled in size.

4. Flatten dough and shape into 6-inch circles. Sprinkle tops evenly with the cornmeal.

5. Place dough on hot grill, cornmeal side down first. Cook for 3 to 4 minutes on each side, until the bread puffs and cooks through. ✄

ROASTED GARLIC
6 heads garlic
¼ cup olive oil

METHOD

1. Preheat oven to 300 degrees.

2. Cut each head of garlic to expose the top of each clove and place in a baking pan. Drizzle liberally with olive oil.

3. Cover pan with foil and place in oven. Bake for one hour or so, until the garlic is tender.

4. Squeeze the soft, roasted garlic out of the clove and spread on the grilled flatbread. ✄

Fog-Mex Chicken Burrito

If you are a Mexican food fan — as we both are — you
know it is difficult to find good Mexican dishes in this
part of the country. We are confident you will enjoy our
version of this popular recipe.

Yields 8 servings

INGREDIENTS

MARINADE

1 cup tomato juice

2 ounces fresh-squeezed lime juice

1 tablespoon garlic, minced

1 tablespoon fresh cilantro,
chopped

1 teaspoon ground cumin

1 teaspoon chili powder

1 tablespoon Fog Island Smokey
Hot Sauce

½ teaspoon Fog Island Real Hot
Sauce

BURRITO

2 pounds chicken breasts, boneless and skinless

2 tablespoons vegetable oil

2 medium onions, sliced

1 green pepper, sliced

1 red pepper, sliced

1½ cups ranchero sauce (p. 20)

½ cup Fog Island Fresh Tomato
Salsa

1 tablespoon fresh cilantro,
chopped

8 large flour tortillas

4 cups grated Monterey Jack or
Cheddar cheese

6 to 8 cups Spicy Black Beans,
warmed (p. 82)

Serve with sour cream, guacamole,
chopped scallions, and Fog
Island Fresh Tomato Salsa

METHOD

1. In a mixing bowl, thoroughly
combine the marinade
ingredients.

2. Place chicken breasts in a
shallow container and pour
marinade over them. Allow
chicken to marinate at least 30
minutes before grilling.

3. Grill chicken on both sides, until
cooked through. Remove from
heat and slice thinly.

4. Heat vegetable oil in a large
saucepan and add sliced onions
and peppers. Sauté over
medium heat until the vegetables are tender. Add the ⟡

ranchero sauce, salsa, and cilantro and stir until incorporated.

5. Add chicken and simmer for 5 to 10 minutes. Taste and adjust the seasonings as needed. Remove from heat.

6. On a griddle or in a large sauté pan, warm each tortilla over medium heat for 1 to 2 minutes until soft (do not brown). Distribute filling evenly on each tortilla, roll up, and place on a sheetpan, seam side down.

7. Top with grated cheese and place under broiler for a few minutes, just until the cheese is melted. Serve burritos on warmed plates with hot black beans. Garnish with dollop of sour cream, guacamole, and salsa and sprinkle with chopped scallions. ✖

GRILLED MARINATED VEGETABLES

On our lunch menu we offer a Mediterranean Veggie Rollup,
which incorporates these grilled marinated vegetables into a
sandwich with pesto and melted mozzarella, rolled in a
warmed tomato tortilla.

Yields 4 to 6 servings

INGREDIENTS

MARINADE

1 cup balsamic vinegar
¼ cup olive oil
1 tablespoon garlic, minced
2 teaspoons Fog Island Stone
   Ground Mustard
½ teaspoon oregano
1 teaspoon basil

VEGETABLES

1 large eggplant, sliced
1 green pepper, sliced
1 red pepper, sliced
1 zucchini, sliced
1 yellow squash, sliced
2 tomatoes, sliced

METHOD

1. Place vinegar, oil, garlic,
   mustard, oregano, and basil in a
   mixing bowl, and whisk together
   until well blended.

2. Toss vegetables in the marinade
   to coat evenly.

3. Cook on a hot grill until the skin
   (if any) bubbles and the
   vegetables are tender and
   thoroughly cooked.

4. Remove from grill and serve
   immediately ✴

HONEY GRAIN MUSTARD

We are big mustard fans at Fog Island, and this recipe is pretty tough to beat. The preparation is a bit involved, not to mention somewhat dangerous, but it is a delicious condiment that is hard to do without once you're hooked.

Yields a little over 4 cups

INGREDIENTS

¾ cup Coleman's dry mustard
¾ cup red wine vinegar
¾ cup dark Karo syrup
½ cup granulated sugar
3 tablespoons honey

1 tablespoon molasses
4 eggs
⅔ cup grain mustard (seeds included)

METHOD

1. In a large bowl, whisk together the Coleman's mustard, vinegar, Karo syrup, sugar, honey, and molasses. Stir well to remove lumps.

2. Cover and let mixture sit overnight.

3. Pour mixture into a heavy gauge saucepan and whisk in eggs. Place on stove and cook over high heat, stirring constantly.

Be careful—the mustard mixture gets very hot! Once the mustard reaches a rapid boil, continue to cook for an additional 5 minutes.

4. Remove from heat and cool to room temperature. Stir in grain mustard and mix thoroughly.

5. Refrigerate until ready to use. ✖

LINGUINE WITH NANTUCKET BAY SCALLOPS

November 1st is always a big day on Nantucket . . .
the opening day of scallop season! We often celebrate
by preparing this luscious pasta dish, which is
actually quite simple to prepare.

Yields 4 servings

INGREDIENTS

2 tablespoons butter
1½ pounds Nantucket bay scallops
1½ cups dry white wine
1 teaspoon garlic, minced
1½ cups heavy cream
¼ cup lemon juice
3 tablespoons freshly grated
  Parmesan cheese
½ cup spinach, washed and

chopped
Salt and pepper, to taste
1 pound fresh linguine (if flavored
  pasta is available, ½ pound
  lemon linguine and ½ pound
  spinach linguine)
2 tablespoons parsley, finely
  chopped

METHOD

1. Heat butter in a large sauté pan. Add scallops and sauté over high heat until scallops are golden brown and natural sugars begin to caramelize, about 5 minutes. Be careful not to overcook or the scallops will become rubbery. Remove scallops to a separate bowl.

2. Add garlic to the pan and cook over medium heat for a minute or so, but do not let the garlic brown. Add white wine and deglaze the pan. Add heavy cream and bring sauce to a simmer. Continue to cook until the sauce reduces by half. Meanwhile, in a large pot, bring 3 to 4 quarts of water to a boil, to cook linguine.

3. Stir lemon juice and Parmesan cheese into simmering sauce and allow to simmer for another 5 to 10 minutes, until sauce is thickened. Add chopped, fresh spinach and season with salt and pepper to taste. Remove pan from heat.

4. Cook linguine in boiling water until al dente. Drain well.

5. Return the sauce to a simmer. Add the cooked pasta and sautéed scallops and stir until combined.

6. Place on warm plates and garnish with freshly chopped parsley. Serve immediately. ✖

Nantucket Fish Cakes

Seafood is plentiful on Nantucket and as a result Islanders are often looking for tasty seafood recipes. Fishcakes make an excellent dinner appetizer and at the Cafe we have served them as a lunch sandwich special on a toasted bun with shredded lettuce and a fresh dill and lemon sauce.

Yields 6 to 8 Servings

INGREDIENTS

2 pounds whitefish fillets such as cod, bass, or halibut
3 tablespoons clarified butter (p. 6)
½ cup onion, finely diced
½ cup green pepper, finely diced
½ cup red pepper, finely diced
¼ cup scallions, finely diced
4 cups breadcrumbs, finely chopped
2 lemons, juiced
2 eggs

¼ cup parsley, finely chopped
2 tablespoons fresh basil leaves, finely chopped (fresh dill may be substituted)
Salt and black pepper to taste
Fog Island Real Hot Sauce, to taste

½ cup clarified butter (p. 6)
Tomato Basil Coulis (see next page)

METHOD

1. Poach fish for 6 to 8 minutes, until cooked. Remove from poaching liquid and set aside to cool.

2. In a medium saucepot, boil potatoes until cooked. Remove from heat, mash, and set aside.

3. In a large sauté pan, heat clarified butter over medium heat. Add onion, green and red peppers, and scallions and cook until tender. Remove from heat and place in a large mixing bowl.

4. Add breadcrumbs, lemon juice, eggs, parsley, and basil. Stir mixture until combined.

5. Flake in the cooked whitefish and stir gently until evenly distributed. Season with salt and black pepper and a dash of Fog Island Real Hot Sauce to taste. ↗

6. Shape fishcake mixture into round patties and place on small sheet-pan. Place in freezer for 20 to 30 minutes to chill. This step helps the fish cakes hold together when they are sauteéd to order.

7. In a large sauté pan or skillet, heat clarified butter. Add fishcakes and panfry over medium heat until golden brown. Turn fishcakes over with a spatula and continue to cook on the second side until evenly brown. Remove from pan and serve at once with tomato basil coulis. ✖

TOMATO BASIL COULIS

The flavors of fresh basil, garden tomatoes, and garlic blend together beautifully to make a delicious sauce that is also great served with pasta.

Yields 6 cups

INGREDIENTS

½ cup onion, minced
1 tablespoon garlic, minced
1 to 2 tablespoons olive oil
8 ounces tomato paste
3 pounds plum tomatoes, peeled, seeded, and diced
3 cups vegetable stock (p. 91)
3 tablespoons fresh basil leaves, finely chopped
½ teaspoon salt
¼ teaspoon black pepper

METHOD

1. In a medium saucepan, sauté onions and garlic in olive oil until the onions are translucent.

2. Stir in tomato paste and sauté over medium heat until the sauce becomes rusty in color.

3. Add tomatoes and vegetable stock and allow sauce to simmer uncovered for about 1 hour, stirring occasionally.

4. Add basil, salt, and pepper and continue to simmer another 20 to 30 minutes to intensify flavors and reduce to proper consistency.

5. Pureé sauce in food processor until smooth. Taste and adjust seasoning as needed. ✖

Portabello Mushroom Burgers

Grilled marinated portabellos are a great vegetarian
alternative to the traditional American hamburger.
Try this recipe at your next cookout.

Yields 6 serving

INGREDIENTS

MARINADE

1 cup balsamic vinegar
¼ cup olive oil
1½ teaspoons Fog Island Stone
   Ground Mustard
1 teaspoon garlic, minced
1 teaspoon rosemary
Fresh ground pepper, to taste

MUSHROOM BURGERS

6 large portabello mushroom caps
6 burger buns
6 slices mozzarella (optional)
12 slices tomato
6 large leaves red leaf lettuce

METHOD

1. In a mixing bowl, whisk together until well blended vinegar, oil, mustard, garlic, rosemary, and pepper.

2. Add mushroom caps to the marinade, making sure they are coated evenly. Let sit in marinade for at least 30 minutes.

3. Grill on both sides until mushroom is fully cooked, about 5 to 8 minutes, depending on size and thickness. Place cheese slices on the mushrooms and melt.

4. Serve on toasted burger buns and garnish as you would a hamburger. ✄

Roasted Veggie Lasagna

This lasagna is loaded with veggies and so tasty
that no one will miss the meat.

Yields 8 servings

INGREDIENTS

SAUCE

1 tablespoon olive oil
1 cup onion, minced
1 tablespoon garlic, minced
1 cup portabello mushrooms,
    finely chopped
1 can crushed tomatoes (28
    ounces)
½ cup parsley, chopped
2 tablespoons pesto (p. 25)
½ cup Parmesan, grated
2 teaspoons oregano

Salt and black pepper, to taste

LASAGNA

16 ounces nonfat ricotta
½ pound spinach, steamed,
    drained, and chopped
18 lasagna noodles, cooked and
    drained
1 recipe grilled marinated vegeta-
    bles (p. 75)
8 ounces nonfat mozzarella, grated

METHOD

1. In a saucepan, heat olive oil over medium heat. Add onion and garlic and sauté until transparent, about 5 to 7 minutes. Add mushrooms and cook for another 3 to 5 minutes.

2. Stir in tomatoes, parsley, pesto, Parmesan, and oregano and simmer for 20 to 30 minutes. Taste sauce and adjust seasonings as needed.

3. In a medium bowl, combine ricotta with cooked spinach and stir until blended.

4. Preheat oven to 350 degrees.

5. Spread some sauce on the bottom of a 13 x 9-inch baking dish. Cover with a layer of 6 noodles, half the ricotta filling, and half of the grilled vegetables. Repeat this layering process. Add a final layer of noodles and top with remaining sauce. Sprinkle evenly with grated mozzarella.

6. Cover with foil and bake for 30 minutes. Remove cover, and bake an additional 15 minutes. Remove from oven and let sit for 10 to 15 minutes before cutting to serve. ✖

SPICY BLACK BEANS

Our black beans are probably our biggest claim to fame.
And, we might add, they are available at every meal we serve.

Yields 8 to 10 servings

INGREDIENTS

4 cups uncooked black beans
4 cups water (adding more as needed)
1 onion, diced
1½ teaspoons garlic, minced
1 tablespoon molasses
2 tablespoons orange juice
1 tablespoon fresh cilantro, chopped

1½ teaspoons chili powder
1½ teaspoons cumin
1½ teaspoons salt, or to taste
1 teaspoon Fog Island Smokey Hot Sauce
¼ teaspoon Fog Island Real Hot Sauce
Sour cream and chopped scallions, for garnish

METHOD

1. Place beans on a sheetpan and carefully sort through to remove small pebbles and impurities.

2. Pour beans into a large pot and cover with water. Soak for at least 4 hours and preferably overnight.

3. Place pot over high heat and bring to a boil. Stir in onions and garlic and reduce the heat. Simmer for several hours, stirring occasionally and adding water so the beans are always covered as they cook.

4. Once the beans have simmered to desired softness, add molasses, orange juice, and seasonings. Continue to cook for another 20 minutes or so to combine flavors and reduce beans to proper consistency. Adjust seasonings to desired taste.

5. Serve hot and garnish with sour cream and chopped scallions. ✶

TABOULLEH SALAD

This popular Middle-Eastern dish is great served as a
salad or as filling for a veggie pita sandwich.

Yields 4 servings

INGREDIENTS

2 cups bulgur

1½ cups hot water

3 to 4 lemons

½ cup tomato juice

4 ripe tomatoes, diced

1 cucumber, peeled and chopped

½ cup scallions, chopped

2 tablespoons olive oil

6 tablespoons fresh mint, chopped

1½ cups parsley, chopped

METHOD

1. Place bulgur in a mixing bowl
   and add hot water. Set aside to
   soak until the water is absorbed
   and the bulgur is softened.

2. Zest 2 lemons and add to bulgur.
   Then juice all the lemons and
   add juice to the bulgur as well.

3. Add remaining ingredients and
   stir until well combined.

4. Chill for several hours and
   serve. ✖

THAI PEANUT SAUCE

This sauce is a key ingredient in one of our signature sandwiches. We char-grill a marinated chicken breast to order, then thinly slice and roll it in a warm flour tortilla with this spicy peanut sauce, shredded carrots, cucumbers, sprouts, and scallions.

Yields 1 1/2 quarts or 5 to 6 cups

INGREDIENTS

1/4 cup vegetable oil

2 tablespoons sesame oil

1 1/2 cups red onion, minced

1/3 cup garlic, minced

1 tablespoon gingerroot, minced

3 tablespoons red wine vinegar

3 tablespoons granulated sugar

2/3 cup ketchup

1 cup hot water

2/3 cup soy sauce

1 tablespoon fresh cilantro, chopped

2 tablespoons lime juice

Dash Fog Island Real Hot Sauce

1 teaspoon black pepper, freshly ground

1 cup chunky peanut butter

METHOD

1. Heat oils and stir in onion, garlic, and ginger. Sauté over medium heat until onions become translucent, about 5 to 7 minutes.

2. Add vinegar and sugar and cook for another 5 minutes until caramel color develops. Stir in ketchup, hot water, and soy sauce and simmer 10 to 15 minutes. Add cilantro, lime juice, hot sauce, and black pepper. Continue to simmer for 5 to 10 minutes longer to blend the flavors and reduce sauce.

3. Remove from heat and let the sauce cool slightly. Stir in peanut butter until fully mixed. Make sure the sauce is not too hot when the peanut butter is added or the sauce will separate. ✄

TURKEY POT PIE

This is a wonderful way to use Thanksgiving leftovers, but please don't be limited to making this dish just once a year.

Yields 8 servings

INGREDIENTS

4 cups turkey or chicken stock
1½ cups onions, diced
1 cup carrots, diced
1 cup celery, sliced on bias
1½ cups potatoes, peeled and
   diced
3 tablespoons cornstarch
½ cup half-and-half
2½ pounds cooked turkey, diced

½ cup peas, frozen
½ cup corn niblets, frozen
2 tablespoons parsley, chopped
1 teaspoon thyme
1 teaspoon basil
½ teaspoon rosemary
Salt and black pepper, to taste
1 recipe pastry dough (p. 68–69)

METHOD

1. In a large saucepan, heat stock to simmering and add onions, carrots, celery, and potatoes. Cook until vegetables are tender, about 15 to 20 minutes.

2. Dissolve cornstarch in the half-and-half and add it to the stock. Bring to a boil to thicken the sauce, stirring frequently, about 10 to 15 minutes.

3. Stir in turkey, peas, corn, and seasonings and cook for an another 5 minutes. Remove from heat and let cool to room temperature.

4. Preheat oven to 375 degrees.

5. Portion the turkey mixture into 6-inch round ceramic casseroles.

6. On a lightly floured surface, roll out pastry dough and cut in circles the size of the casseroles. Place dough on top of casseroles. Press and crimp edges to form a seal. Score or prick dough in a decorative manner to allow the steam to escape during baking.

7. Bake for 20 minutes, until the crust is lightly browned. Remove from oven and serve immediately. ✄

WEST INDIAN CHICKEN CURRY

Great curry dishes can be found all over the islands of the
Caribbean. Specialty food stores often carry imported curry
powders from this region, which tend to be more flavorful
than the generic curry powder from the grocery store.

Yields 6 servings

INGREDIENTS

¼ cup clarified butter (p. 6)

2 onions, diced

4 stalks celery, diced

1 tablespoon garlic, minced

2 tablespoons gingerroot, minced

¼ cup curry powder

⅓ cup all-purpose flour

4 cups chicken stock

2½ to 3 pounds boneless chicken breast, large dice

12 ounces unsweetened coconut milk

2 Granny Smith apples

1 teaspoon Fog Island Real Hot Sauce

Season with salt and freshly ground pepper

6 cups cooked brown rice

Chopped scallions, shredded coconut, and apple slices, for garnish

METHOD

1. In a large saucepan, heat clarified butter and add onions, celery, garlic, and ginger. Cook for several minutes over medium heat until onions become translucent. Stir occasionally.

2. Stir in curry powder and sauté for a minute or so to extract flavor. Add flour and stir in with the vegetables to make a roux.

3. Slowly add chicken stock, stirring continuously to incorporate the roux and avoid lumps.

4. Add diced chicken and bring to a boil. Reduce heat to low, cover and simmer for 30 to 40 minutes, until chicken is tender.

5. Remove the cover and add coconut milk, apples, and hot sauce, stirring until blended. Simmer for 20 to 30 minutes longer to intensify flavors and reduce.

6. Taste and adjust seasonings as needed. Remove from heat and ladle over warm brown rice. Garnish with scallions, shredded coconut, and apple slices. ✶

WILD WEST BARBECUE SAUCE

This sauce is delicious with any barbecued meats,
including chicken, pork, and ribs. We like to serve it as
an alternative to ketchup with char-grilled burgers.

Yields 4 cups

INGREDIENTS

2 tablespoons vegetable oil
1 cup onions, minced
1 tablespoon garlic, minced
1 cup tomato paste
1 tablespoon chili powder
1 cup coffee, strongly brewed
6 tablespoons Worcestershire
   sauce

¾ cup red wine vinegar
¾ cup brown sugar
¾ cup apple cider
1 tablespoon Fog Island Smokey
   Hot Sauce
1 teaspoon Fog Island Real Hot
   Sauce
Salt and black pepper, to taste

METHOD

1. Heat vegetable oil in a saucepan
   and add onions and garlic. Sauté
   over medium heat until onions
   are translucent, about 5 to
   7 minutes.

2. Add tomato paste and continue
   to cook over medium heat,
   stirring continuously, until the
   mixture takes on a rusty color.

3. Add remaining ingredients and
   simmer for 20 to 30 minutes to
   intensify flavors and reduce to
   thicker consistency.

4. Taste and adjust seasonings as
   needed. ✖

IV
SOUP FAVORITES

In the wintertime, as early as 8:00 AM, the telephone
at the Cafe begins to ring with calls from our "regulars"
inquiring, "What soups will you be serving today?"

Our daily lunch menu features "Different Soups
Every Day" along with the popular Beef and Black
Bean Chili and New England Clam Chowder.
We are not only flattered by the enthusiastic
following of the local soup aficionados but thrilled
with the challenge to create new winning recipes.

Over time, we have created a large repertoire
of soups and stews and are happy to share this
selection of requested favorites.

Basic Stocks

We recommend making batches of homemade stock whenever possible. When buying prepared stocks, broths or bases, always read the labels before purchasing to find a brand that is not filled with food additives and flavor "enhancers" such as monosodium glutamate.

BASIC VEGETABLE STOCK

At the Cafe we do not always follow a "recipe" for veggie stock. We have a plastic bin in the refrigerator, so whenever vegetables are prepped, we save the trimmings for stock and make up a large batch every day or two.

Usually the trimmings include onions, carrots, celery, squash, tomatoes, mushrooms, peppers, spinach, leeks, scallions, and stems from fresh herbs.

We don't include certain vegetables that make the stock bitter or lend a peculiar flavor, such as broccoli, asparagus, onion peels, turnips, and cabbage.

If you find yourself cooking for a large family or preparing vegetables quite frequently, you may consider starting your own veggie stock starter bin at home.

If you do not have a lot of trimmings at your disposal, here is a recipe for a flavorful stock.

Yields about 2 quarts

INGREDIENTS
6 large onions, diced
3 leeks, cleaned and sliced
8 carrots, diced
8 stalks celery, diced
4 tomatoes, roughly chopped
½ pound mushrooms
2 scallions, sliced
2½ quarts water
2 bay leaves
1 teaspoon black peppercorn, cracked
6 sprigs parsley
Fresh herbs, if available, such as basil, thyme, parsley, or chives
Salt and pepper, to taste

METHOD
1. Combine all ingredients in a large stockpot and bring to a boil. Reduce heat and gently simmer uncovered for 35 to 45 minutes.

2. Strain the broth and discard the vegetables.

3. Season to taste, depending on desired use.

4. Cool rapidly. Stores for up to 7 to 10 days in refrigerator. ✖

BASIC CHICKEN STOCK
Yields about 2 quarts

INGREDIENTS

4 pounds chicken bones, ask at
    meat counter
1 onion, diced
2 carrots, diced
2 stalks celery, diced
3 quarts water
1 bay leaf
4 sprigs parsley
Pinch thyme

METHOD

1. Place chicken bones in a large
   stockpot with onion, carrots, and
   celery and pour in the water.
   Quickly bring stock to a boil, then
   reduce heat. Simmer uncovered
   for 2½ to 3 hours, periodically
   removing the residue that collects
   on the surface.

2. One hour before the stock has
   completed cooking, add the bay
   leaf, parsley, and thyme.

3. Once the stock has finished
   cooking, strain the liquid.
   Discard bones and vegetables.

4. Cool rapidly. Stores for up to
   7 to 10 days in refrigerator. ✄

BASIC FISH STOCK
Yields about 2½ quarts

INGREDIENTS

1 tablespoon butter
2 large onions, diced
2 leeks, cleaned and sliced
4 stalks celery, diced
6 pounds fish frames from white-
    fleshed fish such as cod or
    haddock, ask at fish counter
3 quarts water
1 bay leaf

METHOD

1. Clean fish bones, removing guts,
   gills, and any blood spots.

2. In a stockpot, sauté onions,
   leeks, and celery in butter on
   low heat until onions become
   translucent, about 5 to 7
   minutes.

3. Add fish bones and cover the
   pot. Over low heat, steam the
   fish bones until the meat is
   white.

4. Add water and bay leaf and bring
   to a boil. Reduce heat and gently
   simmer uncovered for about
   30 minutes. Periodically skim
   residue from the top to eliminate
   impurities.

5. Once the stock has finished
   cooking, strain the liquid.
   Discard bones and vegetables.

6. Cool rapidly. Stores for up to
   7 to 10 days in refrigerator. ✄

ASIAN VEGETABLE SOUP

Highly recommended as a home remedy for head colds . . .
a bowl of this does wonders to clear out the sinuses.
If you don't have a cold—enjoy this vegetarian version
of the classic Chinese hot and sour soup.

Yields 10 to 12 servings

INGREDIENTS

1 teaspoon sesame oil
2 teaspoons vegetable oil
¾ cup onions, sliced
1 tablespoon garlic, minced
1 tablespoon gingerroot, minced
½ cup celery, sliced on bias
½ cup carrots, sliced on bias
½ cup yellow squash, diced
½ cup red pepper, diced
3 quarts vegetable stock (p. 91)
⅓ cup soy sauce

⅓ cup rice wine vinegar
1 tablespoon fresh cilantro, chopped
2 teaspoons toasted sesame oil
Dash Fog Island Real Hot Sauce
1 cup asparagus, sliced diagonally
⅓ cup scallions, chopped
1 cup bean sprouts
1 cup snow peas, sliced diagonally
4 ounces canned water chestnuts, sliced
Salt and black pepper, to taste

METHOD

1. Heat sesame oil and vegetable oil in a 4-quart saucepot over medium heat. Add onions, garlic, ginger, celery, carrots, yellow squash, and red pepper and sauté for several minutes until the vegetables become tender.

2. Add vegetable stock, soy sauce, rice wine vinegar, and cilantro and bring to a boil. Reduce heat and simmer uncovered 15 to 20 minutes to intensify flavors. Stir in sesame oil and dash of Fog Island Real Hot Sauce. Taste and adjust seasoning as needed.

3. Add the asparagus, scallions, bean sprouts, snow peas, and water chestnuts, stirring to mix. Simmer for 5 to 10 minutes, until vegetables are al dente. Be careful not to overcook—one of the great appeals of this soup is the vibrant contrast of colors and freshness of the vegetables.

4. Season to taste with salt and pepper and serve immediately. ✤

93

BEEF AND BLACK BEAN CHILI

This spicy chili, one of our signature items at the Cafe,
is very popular with our year-round customers. We also
serve a tasty vegetarian version, which substitutes bulgur
wheat and corn niblets for the ground beef.

Yields 10 to 12 servings

INGREDIENTS

2½ pounds lean ground beef
½ teaspoon salt
1 teaspoon ground black pepper
1 tablespoon garlic, minced
1 large onion, diced
1 large green pepper, medium dice
1 tablespoon ground chili powder
1 tablespoon ground cumin
1 yellow squash, medium dice
1 zucchini, medium dice
3 cups crushed tomatoes (28 oz. can)

1½ cups water
1½ cups kidney beans (15½ oz. can)
3 cups cooked black beans*
1 tablespoon fresh cilantro, chopped
½ teaspoon Fog Island Real Hot
  Sauce
2 teaspoons Fog Island Smokey
  Hot Sauce
Salt and black pepper, to taste
Sour cream and chopped scallions,
  for garnish

METHOD

1. Add ground beef to a large sauce-pan, and cook over medium heat. Stir meat with a spoon, breaking it into small pieces. Season with salt and black pepper and cook until the meat loses its pink color, about 10 to 15 minutes.

2. Remove from heat and drain off any excess fat as needed. Return meat to the stove and add garlic, onion, and green pepper. Continue to cook over medium heat for 5 to 7 minutes, stirring periodically. ↗

At the Cafe we always have cooked and seasoned black beans on hand since we serve them with many of our dishes. The recipe can be found on page 82. If you do not have cooked beans at your disposal, here's what to do: In a saucepan, soak 1½ cups of black beans in 4 cups of water for at least 4 hours, and preferably overnight. Simmer the beans over medium heat for 1 hour, until the beans are soft, stirring occasionally. Periodically add water, making sure the beans are covered with water as they cook. When the beans are tender, drain off excess liquid and add to the chili.

3. Stir in chili powder and cumin and sauté for a minute to extract the flavors.

4. Add yellow squash and zucchini, crushed tomatoes, water, kidney beans, and cooked black beans, stirring to incorporate. Season with chopped cilantro and Fog Island hot sauces. Simmer uncovered for another 30 to 40 minutes until the vegetables and beans are tender and the flavors are well blended.

5. Taste and adjust seasoning as needed. Garnish with a dollop of sour cream and freshly chopped scallions. ✖

VEGETARIAN CHILI

Fog Island's Sous Chef Sharon Mehrman inspired this vegetarian version of our popular chili recipe.

Follow the same recipe for Beef and Black Bean Chili but eliminate the ground beef.

ADDITIONAL INGREDIENTS

1 cup bulgur
1 cup tomato juice
2 tablespoons olive oil
1 carrot, peeled and diced
1 cup corn niblets

METHOD

1. Place the bulgur in a small bowl and add tomato juice. Set aside to soak.

2. In a large saucepan, heat olive oil, then add onions, garlic, green pepper, and carrots.

3. Stir in chili powder and cumin and sauté to extract the flavors.

4. Add yellow squash and zucchini, crushed tomatoes, corn niblets, water, kidney beans, and cooked black beans, stirring to mix. Season with chopped cilantro and Fog Island hot sauces and simmer uncovered another 30 to 40 minutes, until vegetables and beans are tender and the flavors are well blended.

5. Stir in soaked bulgur and remove from heat. Taste and adjust seasoning as needed. Garnish with freshly chopped scallions. ✖

BROCCOLI AND
VERMONT CHEDDAR SOUP

This is a thick and hearty soup, wonderful with or
without the cream, and one of our personal favorites.

Yields 8 to 10 servings

INGREDIENTS

2 tablespoons clarified butter (p. 6)

1 cup onions, diced

1 tablespoon garlic, minced

2 pounds broccoli (dice stems and set aside flowerettes)

2 large potatoes, peeled and diced

4 quarts vegetable stock (p. 91)

2 teaspoons Fog Island Stone Ground Mustard (or other

Dijon-style mustard)

¼ teaspoon ground white pepper

¼ teaspoon dried leaf thyme

¼ teaspoon dried basil

3 cups grated sharp Cheddar cheese

1 cup half-and-half or light cream (optional)

Salt, to taste

METHOD

1. In a stockpot, sauté onions and garlic in clarified butter over medium heat until translucent, about 5 to 7 minutes.

2. Stir in diced broccoli stems and potatoes. Add vegetable stock and simmer uncovered for 20 to 30 minutes, until broccoli is tender.

3. Remove from heat and allow to cool. Puree in a blender or food processor in batches until a smooth consistency is obtained.

4. Return soup to the stove and bring to a boil. Stir in mustard, pepper, thyme, and basil. Reduce heat and simmer uncovered for 20 to 30 minutes longer, until the soup reduces to desired consistency.

5. Gradually add grated cheese, stirring well to blend.

6. Once the cheese is fully blended, add broccoli flowerettes for a garnish and simmer uncovered an additional 5 to 10 minutes, until broccoli is tender. Be careful not to overcook; the broccoli should be somewhat crisp and bright green.

7. Finish by stirring in the cream, if desired, before serving. Taste and adjust seasoning. ✹

BUTTERNUT SQUASH BISQUE

Because of its hard skin, peeling butternut squash is a tedious
task. For convenience and to save preparation time, look for
butternut squash that is already peeled—in the produce
section of your favorite grocery store.

Yields 8 to 10 servings

INGREDIENTS

2 tablespoons clarified butter (p. 6)
1 cup onion, diced
1 tablespoon garlic, minced
1 tablespoon gingerroot, minced
2 quarts vegetable stock (p. 91)
3 pounds butternut squash, peeled
  and diced

⅓ cup orange juice
½ teaspoon ground cinnamon
¼ teaspoon ground nutmeg
¼ teaspoon ground white pepper
Salt, to taste
⅔ cup half-and-half or light cream
  (optional)

METHOD

1. In a stockpot, sauté onions,
   garlic, and ginger in clarified
   butter over medium heat until
   tender, but do not brown, about
   5 to 7 minutes.

2. Add vegetable stock and
   butternut squash and bring the
   liquid to a boil. Reduce heat and
   simmer uncovered for 20 to 30
   minutes, until squash is very
   soft.

3. Remove from heat and allow to
   cool. Puree in a blender or food
   processor until smooth.

4. Return soup to stockpot and
   bring to a boil. Stir in orange
   juice and season with cinnamon,
   nutmeg, and white pepper.
   Reduce heat and simmer
   uncovered for 20 to 30 minutes
   longer, until the soup reduces to
   the desired consistency.

5. Taste and adjust seasoning as
   needed. Finish by adding the
   cream, if desired, just before
   serving. ✂

CARROT GINGER SOUP

We have received countless requests for this recipe and
promised our soup fans that the recipe would be included
in our first cookbook. Here it is . . . enjoy!

Yields 6 to 8 servings

INGREDIENTS

2 tablespoons clarified butter (p. 6)
1 cup onion, diced
1 tablespoon garlic, minced
2 tablespoons gingerroot, minced
6 cups vegetable stock (p. 91)
1½ pound carrots, chopped
1 teaspoon ground cinnamon

½ teaspoon ground nutmeg
¼ cup orange juice
1 cup half-and-half or light cream
  (optional)
1 teaspoon honey (optional, depending on sweetness of carrots)
Salt and white pepper, to taste

METHOD

1. In a large saucepan, sauté
   onions and garlic in butter until
   tender, about 5 to 7 minutes.
   Stir in minced ginger and cook
   another minute to extract flavor.

2. Add vegetable stock and bring to
   a boil. Next add carrots, cinnamon, nutmeg, and orange juice
   and simmer uncovered for 20
   minutes, until carrots are quite
   tender.

3. Remove soup from heat and let
   cool. Puree soup in a food
   processor or blender in batches
   until smooth.

4. Return soup to heat and simmer
   uncovered 20 to 30 minutes,
   until the soup reduces and the
   flavors intensify.

5. Finish by stirring in cream, if
   desired. Taste and season with
   salt and pepper as needed. A bit
   of honey may be added if the
   carrots lack sweetness. ✖

CURRIED CHICKEN SOUP

Another name for this delicious soup is mulligatawny, which is a traditional favorite in India. Surprisingly, we have found this soup sells much better if we call it "Curried Chicken." Perhaps "mulligatawny" is somewhat intimidating?

Yields 6 to 8 servings

INGREDIENTS

1 cup onion, diced
¼ cup celery, diced
¼ cup green pepper, diced
½ cup carrots, diced
1 tablespoon garlic, minced
4 tablespoons clarified butter (p. 6)
3 tablespoons all-purpose flour
1 tablespoon curry powder
2 quarts chicken stock (p. 92)
½ cup uncooked brown rice
2 Granny Smith apples, peeled and diced

1 cup chicken meat, cooked and diced
½ cup unsweetened, shredded coconut
3 tomatoes, peeled, seeded and diced
2 tablespoons parsley, chopped
½ teaspoon leaf thyme
Dash Fog Island Real Hot Sauce
Salt and white pepper, to taste

METHOD

1. In a heavy saucepan, sauté onion, celery, green pepper, carrots, and garlic in clarified butter over medium heat until tender.

2. Stir in flour to make a roux. Cook over low heat for 3 to 5 minutes but do not brown. Add curry powder and cook for a minute or so to extract flavor. Increase heat to high.

3. Add chicken stock, stirring to keep the soup smooth as it thickens. Once the soup reaches the boiling point, reduce heat so soup is at a low simmer.

4. Add rice and cook uncovered for approximately 30 minutes, until the rice is cooked.

5. Stir in diced apples, chicken meat, shredded coconut, and tomatoes. Add parsley, thyme, and hot sauce and simmer uncovered another 10 to 15 minutes, until apples are tender and the soup has reduced.

6. Season with salt and white pepper to desired taste. ✂

FISHERMAN'S STEW

This stew is loaded with fresh seafood and on a chilly autumn evening makes a wonderful meal served with warm French bread.

Yields 6 to 8 servings

INGREDIENTS

2 tablespoons olive oil
1 cup onion, thinly sliced
1 cup green pepper, thinly sliced
½ cup leeks, thinly sliced
¼ cup fennel, thinly sliced
1 tablespoon garlic, minced
2 cups crushed tomatoes
3 cups fish stock (p. 92)
1 cup clam juice
½ cup dry white wine
Pinch saffron
2 bay leaves
½ teaspoon leaf thyme
Dash Fog Island Real Hot Sauce
1 pound white fish, cut into 1-inch chunks (cod, bass, haddock, halibut, or scallops)
12 to 16 medium shrimp, peeled and deveined
12 to 16 mussels (scrub, remove beards and discard any that are open)
2 tablespoons fresh parsley, chopped fine
1 tablespoon fresh basil, chopped fine
Salt and fresh ground pepper, to taste
Croutons and dollop of rouille (see next page ↗), for garnish

METHOD

1. Heat olive oil in a heavy saucepot and add onion, pepper, leeks, fennel, and garlic. Reduce heat to low and allow to simmer gently for about 10 minutes.

2. Add crushed tomatoes, fish stock, clam juice, and wine and bring soup to a boil.

3. Stir in saffron, bay leaves, thyme, and hot sauce and reduce heat. Simmer uncovered for about 30 minutes to blend flavors.

4. Remove the bay leaves. Add fish, shrimp, and mussels and cook uncovered for 5 to 8 minutes, until the fish is just cooked and the mussel shells have opened. Be careful not to overcook. (If you are planning on leftovers, it is a good idea to add fish only to the amount of stock you think ↗

you will be serving at that meal,
to avoid overcooking the fish.)

5. Finish by adding the chopped
parsley and basil and adjust the
seasoning as needed. Ladle the
stew into soup bowls and top with
croutons and a dollop of rouille. ✄

ROUILLE

*A French garlic-mayonnaise
accompaniment that adds flavor to
broth soups.*

Yields approximately 1 cup

INGREDIENTS

¼ cup roasted red pepper, drained
1 tablespoon garlic, minced
2 tablespoons fresh parsley
2 tablespoons fresh basil
2 egg yolks
½ cup bread crumbs, finely ground
½ cup olive oil
Dash Fog Island Real Hot Sauce
Season with salt and black pepper

METHOD

1. Puree roasted red pepper, garlic,
parsley, and basil in a food processor to a smooth consistency

2. Add egg yolks and bread crumbs
and mix together until blended.

3. Slowly add olive oil and mix into
a thick paste.

4. Season with a dash of hot sauce,
salt, and pepper. Refrigerate
until ready to use. Keeps in
refrigerator 7 to 10 days if well
covered. ✄

FOG-STYLE SPLIT PEA SOUP

Our vegetarian version of the hearty winter favorite, this soup is an extremely quick soup to prepare. It is our standby when disaster strikes and we need a kettle of soup in a hurry.

Yields 8 servings

INGREDIENTS

3 quarts vegetable stock (p. 91)
2 cups dried split peas
3 bay leaves
1 teaspoon leaf thyme
1 teaspoon dried basil
2 tablespoons clarified butter (p. 6) or vegetable oil

1 cup leeks, diced
1 cup celery stalks, diced
1 cup carrots, peeled and diced
1 tablespoon garlic, minced
Salt and black pepper, to taste
2 tablespoons parsley, chopped
1 tablespoon chives, chopped

METHOD

1. Bring the vegetable stock to a boil in a large, heavy-gauge soup pot. Add the split peas, bay leaves, thyme, and basil. Reduce to a simmer and cook uncovered for about one hour, until peas become tender. Stir occasionally.

2. In a separate sauté pan, cook leeks, celery, carrots, and garlic in clarified butter over low heat until tender but not browned. Add cooked vegetables to the soup pot, stirring to incorporate. Simmer uncovered for an additional 20 to 30 minutes, continuing to stir occasionally.

3. Remove bay leaves. Taste soup and season with salt and black pepper as needed. Garnish with chopped parsley and chives and serve. ✖

GAZPACHO

This chilled vegetable soup is available daily on our
summertime lunch menu. To achieve the proper texture,
it is important to dice the vegetables by hand, even if it
is very tempting to use a food processor.

Yields 8 servings

INGREDIENTS

¼ cup olive oil
¼ cup red wine vinegar
3 cups tomato juice or V-8 juice
1 cup vegetable stock (p. 91)
1 tablespoon Worcestershire sauce
Dash Fog Island Real Hot Sauce
¼ teaspoon ground cumin
1 teaspoon fresh cilantro, finely
   chopped

2 teaspoons garlic, minced
½ cup red onion, minced
8 ripe tomatoes, diced
2 cucumbers, diced
2 green peppers, diced
1 red pepper, diced
4 bunches scallions, finely sliced
Salt and black pepper, to taste

METHOD

1. In a large bowl whisk together
   olive oil, red wine vinegar,
   tomato juice, and vegetable
   stock. Also stir in the Worcestershire, hot sauce, cumin, cilantro,
   minced garlic, and onion.

2. Add diced tomatoes, cucumbers,
   peppers, and scallions to the
   soup and stir well to combine.

3. Season with salt and black
   pepper and refrigerate for
   several hours before serving.
   Serve very cold in chilled soup
   bowls. ✖

HUNGARIAN BEEF AND PEPPER STEW

One of our first professional cooking experiences was in a restaurant on Cape Cod. All the chefs were from Vienna, Austria, and had trained in many of the great hotels in Europe. They were kind enough to share their cooking secrets, including an authentic recipe for Hungarian Guylas. This soup recipe was inspired by that original recipe.

Yields 6 to 8 servings

INGREDIENTS

2 tablespoons vegetable oil
3 cups onions, finely diced
2 green peppers, sliced
2 red peppers, sliced
1 pound mushrooms, sliced
2 tablespoons garlic, minced
6 to 8 tablespoons Hungarian paprika
2 tablespoons flour
4 ounces tomato paste
4 cups water or beef stock

3 pounds stew beef or boneless chuck meat, diced
1 tablespoon caraway seeds
½ teaspoon leaf thyme
½ teaspoon basil
Dash Fog Island Real Hot Sauce
12 ounces beer or ale
1 cup sour cream
Salt and black pepper, to taste
2 cups cooked egg noodles (optional)

METHOD

1. In a stockpot, sauté onions in the vegetable oil over medium heat until lightly browned. Add peppers, mushrooms, and garlic and cook for several minutes.

2. Add paprika and stir continuously for about 30 seconds to extract flavor. Be careful not to overcook paprika or soup will have slightly bitter flavor.

3. Add flour and stir to make a roux. Then add tomato paste and stir well to incorporate.

4. Slowly whisk in water or beef stock and continue to stir until soup comes to a boil.

5. Add stew meat, spices, and hot sauce and reduce heat. Slowly pour in the beer and simmer uncovered for about 1 hour, until the meat is tender. Continue to reduce, until soup ⟋

reaches the desired consistency and the flavors intensify.

6. Taste and adjust seasoning as needed. Finish by adding sour cream, stirring constantly until well mixed. Stir in egg noodles, if desired, and serve immediately. ✖

MEDITERRANEAN VEGETABLE SOUP

When we serve this soup at Fog Island, customers often ask, "What makes this soup Mediterranean?" Our standard reply is that this soup incorporates ingredients indigenous to the cuisines of this celebrated European coastal region.

Yields 8 servings

INGREDIENTS

¼ cup black-eyed beans, cannellini beans, or other dried beans
3 tablespoons olive oil
1 cup onion, diced
½ cup celery, diced
½ cup carrots, diced
¼ cup green pepper, diced
¼ cup cabbage, julienne-cut
1 cup zucchini or yellow squash, diced

1 tablespoon garlic, minced
2 quarts vegetable stock (p. 91)
1 cup crushed tomatoes
¼ cup ditalini, tubettini (or other small pasta)
½ cup chick-peas
3 tablespoons pesto (p. 27)
Salt and black pepper, to taste
Grated Parmesan cheese, for garnish

METHOD

1. Simmer black-eyed beans in water (enough to cover) for about 2 hours, until cooked. Drain and set aside.

2. In a stockpot, sauté onion, celery, carrots, peppers, cabbage, squash, and garlic in olive oil until tender but not browned, about 10 to 12 minutes.

3. Add vegetable stock and crushed tomatoes. Simmer uncovered for about 15 minutes, being careful not to overcook the vegetables.

4. Add pasta and cook until al dente, about 10 minutes, depending on type of pasta.

5. Stir in the cooked beans, chick-peas, and pesto. Bring to a quick boil and adjust seasoning to taste.

6. Garnish with grated Parmesan cheese and serve immediately. ✖

MEXICAN TORTILLA SOUP

This spicy pepper and tomato soup is the Mexican version of the popular French Onion. Before serving, the soup is garnished with tortilla chips and grated Monterey Jack cheese is melted over the top.

Yields 8 servings

INGREDIENTS

3 tablespoons vegetable oil
1 cup onions, thinly sliced
1 cup green pepper, thinly sliced
2 cups red pepper, thinly sliced
1 tablespoon garlic, minced
6 cups vegetable stock (p. 91)
2 cups crushed tomatoes
2 cups diced tomatoes
2 teaspoons ground cumin
1 tablespoon chili powder
1 tablespoon fresh cilantro, chopped

1 tablespoon Fog Island Smokey Hot Sauce, or to taste
½ teaspoon Fog Island Real Hot Sauce, or to taste
½ cup scallions, sliced
1 cup corn niblets, fresh or frozen
1 tablespoon lime juice (optional)
Salt and pepper, to taste
Tortilla chips and grated Monterey Jack cheese, for garnish

METHOD

1. Heat vegetable oil in a stockpot over low heat. Add onions, peppers, and garlic and cook until the onions become transparent, about 5 to 7 minutes.

2. Add vegetable stock, tomatoes, cumin, chili powder, chopped cilantro, and hot sauces and bring the soup to a boil. Reduce heat and simmer for 15 to 20 minutes.

3. Add scallions and corn niblets. Continue to simmer for an additional 5 to 10 minutes, until the corn is tender.

4. Add lime juice and adjust seasoning to taste.

5. Ladle into individual ovenproof soup terrines. Top each terrine with a layer of tortilla chips and a handful of grated Monterey Jack cheese. Place under a broiler and heat until the cheese melts. Serve at once. ✖

MUSHROOM AND WILD RICE SOUP

Portabello mushrooms are the secret to this
soup's robust mushroom flavor.

Yields 8 to 10 servings

INGREDIENTS

1 tablespoon clarified butter (p. 6)

1 cup onion, diced

2 teaspoons garlic, minced

3 cups portabello mushrooms,
coarsely chopped

2 quarts vegetable stock (p. 91)

1 cup potato, peeled and diced

½ cup wild rice

4 cups mushrooms, sliced (any
variety)

1 cup half-and-half or light cream
(optional)

1½ teaspoons leaf thyme

Salt and black pepper, to taste

METHOD

1. Heat clarified butter in a large saucepan and add onion and garlic. Sauté over medium heat until the onions become tender.

2. Add portabello mushrooms, vegetable stock, and diced potato and bring soup to a boil. Reduce heat and simmer uncovered for about 30 minutes.

3. Remove saucepan from the stove and allow to cool. Puree soup in a blender or food processor to a smooth consistency.

4. Return pureed soup to the saucepan and bring to a boil. Reduce heat and add wild rice and sliced mushrooms. Simmer uncovered for 30 to 40 minutes, until the rice is cooked.

5. Finish by adding the cream, if desired. Be careful not to bring soup to a boil after cream is added. Add thyme and adjust salt and pepper to taste. ✖

OLD-FASHIONED CHICKEN DUMPLING SOUP

This soup certainly fits into the category of "comfort" foods and may remind you of soup Grandma used to make.

Yields 6 to 8 servings

INGREDIENTS

2 tablespoons clarified butter (p. 6)
1 cup onion, diced
1 teaspoon garlic
¾ cup celery, diced
½ cup carrots, diced
2 quarts chicken stock (p. 92)
2 bay leaves

½ teaspoon basil
½ teaspoon leaf thyme
½ teaspoon rosemary
¾ pound chicken meat, cooked and diced
Salt and white pepper, to taste

METHOD

1. In a stockpot, sauté onion, garlic, celery, and carrots in clarified butter until almost tender, about 5 to 7 minutes.

2. Add chicken stock, bay leaves, basil, thyme, and rosemary. Bring to a boil, then reduce heat and simmer uncovered for 15 to 20 minutes.

3. Stir in diced chicken and season to taste with salt and pepper.

4. Make the dumpling batter (see next page).

5. Shape dumplings into round balls using a small, greased ice cream scoop or a tablespoon. Gently drop dumplings into the simmering soup. Cover stockpot and cook for about 15 minutes, until the dumplings are firm.

6. Taste and adjust seasoning as needed. ✄

CHIVE AND BASIL DUMPLINGS
Yields 16 dumplings

INGREDIENTS

1 cup cake flour
2 teaspoons baking powder
½ teaspoon salt
¼ cup fresh chives, chopped
1 tablespoon fresh basil, chopped
¼ cup grated Parmesan cheese
¼ teaspoon chili powder
1 egg
½ cup milk

METHOD

1. Combine flour, baking powder, and salt in a bowl. Mix in chives, basil, Parmesan cheese, and chili powder.

2. Add egg and milk, stirring only enough to moisten the batter. It is important not to overwork the batter so the dumplings will be tender. ✂

Portuguese Kale Soup

Due to the Portuguese influence in many coastal communities in southern New England, this soup is a regional specialty.

Yields 8 to 10 servings

INGREDIENTS

1 pound linguica*
3 tablespoons olive oil
1½ cups onion, diced
1 tablespoon garlic, minced
¾ cup carrots, diced
2 quarts chicken stock (p. 92)
1 pound chef potatoes, scrubbed and diced
~~3 cups crushed tomatoes~~
1½ cups kidney beans, canned
~~1 pound kale, cleaned and chopped~~
Salt and black pepper, to taste
add cilantro, mint

METHOD

1. Prick linguica and blanch in a pot of boiling water for several minutes to eliminate most of the excess fat. Drain linguica and let cool. Cut into ¼-inch thick slices and set aside.

2. In a stockpot, sauté onion, garlic, and carrots in olive oil until tender.

3. Add chicken stock and potatoes. Simmer uncovered for about 20 minutes, until the potatoes are cooked.

4. Remove soup from heat and strain out about half the potatoes and vegetables. Puree in a food processor to give the soup a slightly thicker consistency. Add this pureed mixture back to the soup and return to the heat.

5. Add crushed tomatoes and kidney beans and simmer uncovered for an additional 10 to 15 minutes.

6. Add linguica and kale and continue to simmer uncovered for another 10 minutes, until the kale is cooked.

7. Season with salt and pepper to taste and serve.

* *Linguica is a spicy Portuguese sausage available in the meat section of most grocery stores.*

RED PEPPER CORN CHOWDER

When sweet corn is in season at the local farm, we use
fresh corn kernels scraped right off the cob. However,
this recipe is very tasty using frozen corn niblets when
fresh is unavailable. The addition of fresh dill weed,
which is available year-round, adds a unique flavor.

Yields 8 servings

INGREDIENTS

2 tablespoons clarified butter (p. 6)
1 large onion, diced
1 tablespoon garlic, minced
2 quarts vegetable stock (p. 91)
2 cups red bliss potatoes,
    scrubbed and diced
2 teaspoons fresh dill, chopped

1 teaspoon leaf thyme
½ teaspoon chili powder
4 cups corn niblets
½ cup scallions, sliced
½ cup red pepper, diced
1 cup half-and-half or light cream
Salt and white pepper, to taste

METHOD

1. Heat clarified butter in a stockpot over low heat. Add onion and garlic and cook until transparent, but do not brown.

2. Pour in vegetable stock and add potatoes, dill, thyme, and chili powder. Simmer uncovered for 20 minutes, until potatoes are tender.

3. Add corn niblets and continue to simmer for another 5 minutes. Remove soup from heat and puree one-half of the soup in a blender or food processor. This will give the soup a slightly thicker consistency. Return the pureed soup to the stockpot and place back on the burner.

4. Stir in scallions and red pepper and finish by adding the cream. Simmer for an additional 10 minutes, being careful not to bring soup to a boil once the cream has been added.

5. Season with salt and pepper as needed and serve. ✄

Chowder Base: The chowder freezes remarkably well—4 to 6 weeks well covered—at the stage before the milk and cream are added (Step 4). To use at a future time, simply remove the base from the freezer and thaw. Then heat the base and add scalded milk and cream. Season to taste, and you are in business!

ROASTED POTATO SOUP
WITH GARLIC AND ROSEMARY

A great way to use leftover potatoes—either baked or mashed.
Simply substitute the same quantity of cooked potatoes for the
uncooked potatoes in Step 3 of the recipe.

Yields 8 to 10 servings

INGREDIENTS

1 tablespoon olive oil
2 cups red bliss potatoes,
    scrubbed and diced
6 garlic cloves, skins on
2 tablespoons clarified butter (p. 6)
1 cup onion, diced
1 cup leeks, sliced
6 cups vegetable stock (p. 91)

4 cups potatoes, peeled and diced
2 bay leaves
1 tablespoon rosemary
1 teaspoon leaf thyme
2 tablespoons parsley, chopped
½ cup half-and-half or light cream
    (optional)
Salt and white pepper, to taste

METHOD

1. In a small roasting pan, coat red potatoes and cloves of garlic with olive oil and season with salt and pepper. Roast in a 375 degree oven for 30 to 40 minutes, until potatoes are tender and golden brown. Remove from oven and set aside.

2. In a stockpot, sauté onion and leeks in clarified butter until soft.

3. Cover with vegetable stock and add peeled (uncooked) potatoes along with bay leaves, rosemary, and thyme. Simmer uncovered for about 25 to 30 minutes, until potatoes are soft. Remove from heat and let cool.

4. Remove bay leaves from soup. Next remove skins from the roasted garlic and add garlic to the soup. Puree soup in batches in a blender or food processor until fairly smooth and add back to the stockpot.

5. Return soup to the stove and bring to simmering. Stir in roasted potatoes and chopped parsley.

6. Finish by adding cream and season with salt and pepper to taste. ✖

SHRIMP BISQUE

This soup "flies out the door" every time we make a batch.
Several of our regular customers ask us to give them a call
when Shrimp Bisque is one of our featured soups of the
day, so they can reserve a bowl before it runs out.

Yields 10 to 12 servings

INGREDIENTS

½ cup plus 2 tablespoons clarified butter (p. 6)

2 pounds shrimp, peeled and deveined (fresh rock shrimp is ideal, if available; small popcorn shrimp work well, or whatever is on sale. Large shrimp may be cut to bite-sized pieces.)

Splash of brandy, for deglazing

1 cup onion, finely diced

2 tablespoons garlic, minced

4 teaspoons paprika

1 cup all-purpose flour

6 cups fish stock (p. 92)

2 cups tomato juice

¼ teaspoon white pepper

Dash Fog Island Real Hot Sauce

½ cup dry sherry

4 cups half-and-half or light cream

Salt and white pepper, to taste

METHOD

1. Save the shells if you are peeling and deveining your own shrimp. Sauté shells in a little butter and simmer uncovered in fish stock for 10 to 15 minutes to extract flavor. Remove shells from stock before adding to the soup in Step 5.

2. In a large sauté pan, heat 2 tablespoons clarified butter over high heat. Add shrimp and sauté for several minutes, stirring occasionally, until shrimp is cooked (take care not to overcook). Deglaze pan with a splash of brandy and remove from heat. Drain cooking liquid and set aside for later use (Step 5). Once shrimp has cooled, dice and set aside.

3. In a large saucepot, heat ½ cup clarified butter. Add onion and garlic and cook over medium heat until tender, about 5 to 7 minutes. Add paprika and sauté for a minute or so to extract the flavor, being careful not to burn. ↗

4. Add flour to make a roux, stirring constantly to incorporate. Continue to cook for several minutes over medium heat.

5. Slowly whisk in fish stock, tomato juice, and shrimp cooking liquid, blending well to eliminate lumps. Bring soup to a boil, then reduce heat. Add white pepper, hot sauce, and sherry. Simmer uncovered for 30 to 40 minutes to reduce soup and intensify the flavors.

6. Add cream, stirring to incorporate. Be careful not to bring the soup to a boil once the cream is added.

7. Stir in chopped shrimp. Taste and adjust seasoning to taste. ✖

VEGETARIAN FRENCH ONION SOUP

The secret to this recipe is to caramelize the onions over low heat to extract the sweet, delicate onion flavor. Unlike most French onion soup recipes, we use vegetable stock rather than beef or chicken. The successful creation of this recipe inspired us to eliminate using meat stocks in all our vegetable-based soups at Fog Island.

Yields 8 servings

INGREDIENTS

3 tablespoons clarified butter (p. 6)
3 pounds onions, sliced fine
2 teaspoons garlic, minced
1 tablespoon molasses
1 cup dry white wine
3 quarts vegetable stock (p. 91)
1 teaspoon Fog Island Stone Ground Mustard (or another Dijon-style mustard)
2 bay leaves
½ teaspoon leaf thyme

½ teaspoon rosemary
Dash Fog Island Real Hot Sauce
¼ cup brandy
Salt and freshly ground black pepper, to taste

GARNISH

1½ cups garlic and Parmesan croutons (see next page ⬈)
2 cups grated Swiss cheese

METHOD

1. In a heavy stockpot, heat clarified butter and stir in onions and garlic. Cover and cook over low heat for about 15 minutes, stirring occasionally. Remove cover and continue to caramelize the natural sugars in the onions, cooking for another 30 to 40 minutes. Stir frequently to avoid burning. When finished, the onions should reduce dramatically in volume and be deep brown.

2. Add molasses and continue to stir over heat for another minute or so. Add white wine and deglaze the pan, scraping the caramelized sugars with a spoon.

3. Whisk in vegetable stock and add mustard, herbs, and hot sauce. Bring soup to a boil and reduce heat. Simmer uncovered for about 25 to 30 minutes longer to reduce. ⬈

4. Remove bay leaves and adjust seasoning as needed. Stir in brandy.

5. Ladle soup into individual oven-proof terrines. Top each terrine with a layer of croutons. Sprinkle the grated Swiss cheese on top and place under a broiler. Heat until cheese melts and is slightly golden. ✖

GARLIC CROUTONS
Yields about 2 cups

INGREDIENTS

1 loaf French bread, cut into small cubes
1 tablespoon garlic, minced
½ cup olive oil (or butter)
¼ cup Parmesan cheese, grated

METHOD

1. Place bread cubes on a sheet-pan. Combine minced garlic with olive oil. Slowly drizzle this mixture over bread cubes. Gently toss to evenly distribute. Sprinkle with Parmesan cheese.

2. Toast in a 350 degree oven for approximately 15 minutes, until croutons are golden brown. Remove from oven and set aside to cool. ✖

INDEX

NOTES

NOTES

ABOUT THE AUTHORS

For Mark and Anne Dawson, owning and operating the Fog Island Cafe on Nantucket is a long-time dream they have brought to fruition. The couple first met as students at the Culinary Institute of America in Hyde Park, New York, in 1983. A few years after graduating, they moved to Nantucket and were married on the Island in 1987. Anne and Mark are very familiar with Nantucket's restaurant industry, working in several local establishments before they had the opportunity to open their own restaurant for the Christmas Stroll in 1993.

The couple designed the cafe's interior themselves, aiming for a casual and inviting atmosphere. Hospitality is as important to the Dawsons as the high-quality and healthy menu selections they serve. Fog Island offers breakfast and lunch year-round and is open for dinner as well in-season. For the Dawsons, Nantucket has become their home. They live on the Island year-round with their daughter Sabrina. ✺

ABOUT FOG ISLAND

For those who have not been fortunate enough to visit the beautiful island of Nantucket, 26 miles off the Massachusetts coastline, fog rolling in off the ocean can be a common occurrence, especially in the warmer months of the year. This weather phenomenon often wreaks havoc with vacationers' travel plans, with the unexpected closing of the island airport.

According to the National Climatic Data Institute in Ashville, North Carolina, Nantucket has the foggiest airport on the East Coast of the United States. Islanders simply learn to accept the fog as part of the local charm and develop a fondness for the drone of the harbor's whistle buoy on foggy evenings.

Along with its mystical qualities, the fog also conjures up feelings of romance as in the movie classic, *Casablanca*. As a popular honeymoon destination, many newlyweds seek to experience Nantucket's romantic charm firsthand. We hope you have the good fortune to experience this unique Island. ✺

129

Fog Island
Mail Order Form

SOLD TO

Name_____

Address _____

City/State _____

Zip _____

Phone _____
(In case we have questions about your order)

SHIP TO

Name_____

Address _____

City/State _____

Zip _____

Phone _____

SALES TAX
5% sales tax added if MA is delivery destination. Food & clothes excluded from MA sales tax.

SHIPPING CHARGES *(continental U.S.)*
Shipping and handling charges will be added to your total. Ground transportation is used if no preference is conveyed. Next Day Air and Second Day Air are available.

METHOD OF PAYMENT

❏ My check for US$_____ is enclosed.

❏ My money order for US$_____ is enclosed.

❏ I'd like to pay by credit card:
  ❏ MasterCard
  ❏ Visa

  Card no. _____

  Name _____

  Exp. date _____

  Signature _____

TO ORDER
You have three choices!

1. Photocopy this page and mail to:
Fog Island Cafe
7 South Water Street
Nantucket, MA 02554

2. Order by phone. Call us toll-free:
(888) FOG-ISLE
(888) 364-4753

3. Order on our web page:
www.fogisland.com

Qty	Item	Price	Total
	Fog Island Cookbook *Nantucket Recipes from the Fog Island Cafe*	$14.95	
	Fog Island Sweatshirt (grey) Circle size: L / XL	$24.95	
	Fog Island T-shirt (white; call for other colors) Circle size: L / XL	$15.00	
	Fog Island Hat (white with colored bill) Circle bill color: blue / green / red	$15.00	
	Fog Island Heavy-duty Totebag (blue)	$29.95	
	Special Blend Coffee (1 lb., whole bean)	$9.95	
	Fog Island Golf Balls (3-pack)	$8.95	
	Real Hot Sauce	$5.95	
	Mustard (stone-ground)	$3.95	
	Raspberry Preserves	$4.95	
	Orange Marmalade	$3.95	
	Smokey Hot Sauce	$5.95	
	Granola (1 lb.)	$5.95	
	Breakfast Pack Fog Island Granola, Coffee, Preserves, and Marmalade	$24.95	
	Hot Pack Fog Island Hot Sauce, Smokey Hot Sauce, Mustard, and Salsa	$21.00	
	Golf Pack *The Mystery of Golf* (book), 3 Fog Island Golf Balls (Titlelist), and Golf Towel	$25.00	
		Subtotal	
	MA sales tax *(where appropriate)*		
	Shipping & handling *(see explanation)*		
		TOTAL	

Prices subject to change without notice.